ADAM THE GARDENER

With an introduction and contributions

by Max Davidson

A pictorial calendar and guide to the year's
in the garden, showing how to grow vegeta
fruit and flowers.

This edition published 1994 by Sunburst Books, an imprint of the Promotional Reprint Company Limited, Deacon House, 65 Old Church Street, London Express Newspapers PLC 1994. The right of Express Newspapers PLC to be identified as the author of this work has been asserted to them in accordance with the atents act 1988.
ISBN 1 85778 103 1. Printed and bound in Finland.

CONTENTS

ENJOY YOUR GARDENING

ISN'T it just one of the marvellous things about having an interest in gardening that you can always plan and hope for better times ahead? There is never any need for clouds on our horizons.

Will this summer be as long and as hot as the previous one? Will the sun blaze down and send us all scurrying for shade? There is no good reason why we should not strike lucky two years running. After all, we gardeners are all optimists. Why else would we sow seeds in spring with little encouragement from the weather if we were not *sure* that at least something would come up!

That is the gamble of gardening and, many would agree, three-quarters of the fun.

The other quarter is patience. Some people say that patience is a virtue. It is more than that. It is the secret ingredient of successful gardening: with patience there is no limit to what you can achieve. You can grow magnificent roses, prize-winning vegetables and exotic plants with odd-sounding names; you can have a lawn which is lush and green and the envy of the neighbourhood. But most important of all you can have the deep satisfaction of doing something well and the pride of knowing that you have found success.

You might discover such enjoyment by having a greenhouse. Modern aluminium greenhouses offer first-rate value for money and, because of their construction, give many years of pleasure without trouble or maintenance costs.

With a greenhouse you could have tomatoes, melons and cucumbers as well as being able to give many vegetables (such as cabbage, cauliflower and beans) a flying start indoors before planting them outside. You would be able to have lettuce all year round, as well as being able to raise new potatoes in large pots for lunch at Easter.

If you could provide some heat in the greenhouse, you could grow all sorts of pot plants and half-hardy annuals to fill those bare spots in summer borders. You could have everything from antirrhinums to dwarf pomegranates, and orchids to zinnias. You name it: YOU can grow it if you have a mind to.

It is easy in these times when money is tight to get pressured into digging up the lawn to produce a bigger vegetable patch. But think carefully before you do so. Unless you have a lot of time free, the extra work might be more than you and your back can cope with. Far better to make the most use of your existing arrangements by increasing the productivity of your plot. For instance, runner beans give much greater return for a given growing area than peas, and lettuces are more practical than cauliflowers. Choosing the correct varieties for your particular needs is a great help too. The cabbage lettuce called Tom Thumb provides tight, solid little heads with the very minimum of

4

waste; the cos lettuce Little Gem is also very compact and can be grown 4in. apart in the garden or even a window box! If you find that under hot, dry conditions your lettuces bolt to seed, then growing Lobjoits Green Cos should go most of the way to solving the problem.

However, no matter what you decide to do in the vegetable plot, take time to refer to the appropriate section of this book. You will most likely find the answer to your problem. For that is one thing you can always be sure of in gardening: if you hit a snag, you can be certain someone else has experienced it before.

Do not take too much notice of what you have been told about having to give a lot of space to vegetables. A plot 10ft. wide and 20ft. long will provide most of the vegetables for a family of four for much of the year.

After all, in order to enjoy gardening to the full, you want to be able to grow many different plants and shrubs. More roses, for example. Do you ever think what splendid value a rose bush represents? You can still buy a rose bush for the price of a packet of cigarettes, two pints of beer or half a gallon of petrol. Rose bushes last for years and give you summer after summer of colour and scent. You doubt that roses are as fragrant nowadays as they once were? Have you ever had a sniff of the deep orange-salmon blooms of the floribunda rose Elizabeth of Glamis or the heavily perfumed turkey-red flowers of the hybrid tea Ernest Morse? Of course, if it is scent you are after, you could not do better than to choose some of the magnificent shrub roses such as the "musks" which fill the garden with their fragrance. As the word "shrub" implies, there are roses for general planting and need not be given a bed to themselves. But why stop at the musks, when there are China roses, moss roses, damask and Gallica roses? You could even think about planting a few more climbers and ramblers . . . such as Albertine, with flowers of coppery chamois, fading to rich salmon-pink *and* deliciously scented. Then there is Danse de Feu, a fiery orange-red and marvellous for cheering up a cold north wall. Nowadays there is no such thing as a right and a wrong season for planting roses or any other shrubs, come to that. You can go along to your local nursery or garden centre, collect the shrub which takes your fancy and plant it when the weather is suitable. What could be more sensible or easy than that?

The container revolution is just one of the ways that the drudgery has been taken out of gardening and a lot more pleasure has been put in. If you would like to take the labour-saving idea a little further, why not lay out a portion of your garden so that it will take care of itself? Heathers are ideal for this purpose. With a suitable selection you can have them in flower from January to December. And the winter-flowering kinds, especially, are tolerant of most soils and situations. With heathers you can plant some of the very attractive dwarf conifers which add interest and colour to the garden all year but particularly in the bleak days of winter. You can have conifers like the blue Boulevard and the gold and bronze Rheingold. If your soil is suitable, there is also the delight of having orange and scarlet azaleas to brighten April and May days. And your labour-saving bed, with its weed-suppressing mat of heathers, can be under-planted with dwarf daffodils for spring and the occasional exotic lily for summer.

If cutting down on the work you have to do in your garden is your aim this year, you could not do better than to think about buying a new lawn-mower. There are some marvellous machines available nowadays from the airborne hover types to electrically powered cylinder mowers. What kind should you choose? If you live in an area of high rainfall, a rotary mower is the best bet, either with a grass collection box or without in the case of the hover mower which chews the grass so finely that no collection is necessary—if the grass is cut often enough. Many modern mowers have rear-mounted grass collection boxes to save you having to empty them so often and also to enable you to mow closer to flower beds. However, if your lawn is your pride and joy, you cannot do better than to buy either a petrol-powered or electric cylinder mower. British mowers are superb. Is it any wonder that foreigners talk in awe about an English lawn?

Yet it is a sad fact that, despite our reputation as garden lovers, we spend a miserly £10 a year per household on our gardens. Perhaps now is not the time to do much about that, but are you getting good value for your money? For instance, have you ever made use of some of the modern varieties of easy-to-sow pelleted seeds to raise new and more colourful plants for your garden? Outdoors in June, in a sheltered corner, you could raise columbines, lupins, delphiniums, wallflowers and pansies, all for a few pence.

In fact, if you wish, you could quite easily raise any one of the many hardy perennial plants. There is no need to stick to the safe and usual ones. What about achillea, chelone, echinops, heuchera, liatris and tritoma? Some superior varieties are usally only available if grown from seed. For example, there is Rudbeckia Marmalade, which is treated as a biennial and sown in June to provide plants to flower the following year. It has flowers of a glorious golden orange and it keeps on flowering from summer into late autumn. As it is only 15in. high, it needs no staking and is a great performer.

You can also raise many superb shrubs from seed to save money. There are brooms in shades of pink, orange and crimson, dwarf lavender as well as buddleia, daphne, kalmia and pieris.

If you do nothing else this year, do resolve to try something new, whether it be alpine strawberries or juicy, home-grown cantaloupe melons.

Give a thought to having water in your garden to make it sparkle. With a pool you can have some of the most beautiful plants in the world . . . the water lilies . . . as well as colourful fish like blue shubunkins and fantail goldfish. And by making use of a plastic pool liner you could complete the entire job of construction and planting the pool in a couple of leisurely weekends.

There are some great times ahead for you in the garden. What fun you are going to have in the months to come with new things to do and plans to be made. Each little success will spur you on to greater effort; each triumph will bring joy.

Happy gardening!

SOWING SWEET-PEAS

The earliest sweet-peas to flower in the garden are those sown in September, but if you did not sow any then you can do so now, under glass. Incidentally if you did sow in September, the plants should now be ready for stopping—that is, pinching out the growing tip so that the plants make new shoots from the base.

To return to the sowing of seeds now, in a greenhouse or frame or, perhaps, in a conservatory on the south side of the house.

One of the problems is to ensure that the skin on all the seeds splits to allow germination. It is therefore wise to soak the seeds in water for 24 hours before sowing. If, after this, some of the seeds have not opened, split the skin with a pen-knife, as shown in inset A, on the side of the seed opposite the growing point, taking care not to harm the body of the seed under the skin.

You can use the John Innes or other suitable compost if you wish; but if you want to make up your own, mix 3 parts of turfy loam, 1 part leafmould and 1 part sharp sand together. Mix it thoroughly and make it evenly moist. Then you can sow the seeds individually in containers such as the egg cases shown in inset B or 5 to a 5-inch pot as in inset C. Assuming your compost is nicely moist, don't water them for two days. Cover the pots, etc., with glass and paper to keep them dark until the seeds germinate. Then remove all cover so that they have plenty of ventilation and keep the compost nicely moist at all times from now on.

When the plants are a reasonable size to handle they will need potting on and when three pairs of leaves have formed the growing tips should be removed to make the seedlings branch out, as mentioned earlier for the September-sown ones.

When the plants are 3 to 4 in. high they can be planted outside, usually in March or April, at which time a sowing can be made in the open garden in order to extend the flowering period, which will then go on until October probably.

CARNATION CUTTINGS

One of the joys of a greenhouse, apart from the fact that you can continue gardening inside it when work outside is impossible, is that it enables you to have plants in bloom all the year round. Normally, this is achieved with plants of different kinds, but with perpetual carnations you can achieve it with just the one flower. Moreover, it is almost expense-less as you simply continue taking cuttings at intervals from adult plants, generation after generation as it were.

You can start now and carry on doing so month after month until about May or June. Even if you do not possess a "parent" plant to start with, a friend will usually oblige with a few cuttings. But be sure you get good healthy stock. If you are in any doubt, and give-aways can at times be rather "ribby", order some from a specialist.

The inset shows the ideal cutting. It should be about 4 in. long and taken from the centre of a plant. You cannot always get them this length. An inch or so either way isn't all that important, so don't discard those that are not the ideal length. Remove each cutting with a "heel" of the old stem attached but trim off any skin of the heel over half an inch long. Also remove the lower leaves.

Fill the pots with equal parts of loam, peat and sand, moderately watered. Dip the end of each cutting in water and then in a hormone rooting powder. Make a hole for each one with a pencil round the edge of the pot of compost, pop in the cutting and make firm with your fingers. Four or five a pot is about right.

They should then go into a propagating case in the greenhouse with bottom heat if possible at a temperature of about 50°F (10°C). Keep them carefully watered until rooted, then pot up singly, first in 3 in. pots and later into 5 in. pots. The mixture for these pots is light loam 4 parts, leafmould and sand 1 part each, plus bone-meal 4 ozs. to the bushel of soil, or a dressing of carnation fertiliser. The mixture must be light enough to drain well. Add more sand if considered necessary.

Pinch out the growing point several times, to produce bushy plants, until late June, then stand the pots out-of-doors for the summer.

A SPECIAL CLIMBER

I am often asked by readers to recommend a climbing plant that will, in effect, be all things to all men. In other words, it must be hardy, must be evergreen so that it is still a screen in winter-time, should have attractive foliage, plus large, exotic flowers, etc., etc. Well, here's the answer to most of those gardeners' prayers.

To those people who know it, it is usually called Trumpet Creeper or Trumpet Bloom, a reference to the shape of the flowers. In catalogues, it is nowadays usually called Campsis radicans but not so long ago it was called Tecoma and Bignonia—just to make it more difficult to find! Campsis includes both greenhouse and hardy kinds, so make sure you get the right one—C. Radicans, the hardy climber that produces great numbers of its orangy-red trumpets from July to September if it has its best position—a south or west facing wall, fence, old tree, pergola support, or anything else it can happily ramble over. You can even grow it in a pot—preferably a 9 in. one—so that it can festoon your new conservatory or sun lounge.

Having, I hope, whetted your appetite, now is the time to sow the seed, up to the beginning of March. It needs doing now because the seeds need stratification, which means exposing the seed-box to frost.

Almost fill a seed-box with a good seed compost such as John Innes in the usual way. I don't favour a soil-less compost for this job. Sprinkle the seed on top and cover with a light sprinkling of compost or sand.

Place the box out-of-doors for a month, then bring it into a greenhouse or propagating frame where it needs 70°F. (21°C.) and should be kept in shade.

When large enough, transplant into 3 in. pots. By late summer the plants will be large enough to put out in the garden but protect them if we should get a cold spell until they are fully established. Remove any flower-buds that form the first year to make the plant concentrate on growth.

EARLY STRAWBERRIES

The month of January may seem a strange time to be writing about strawberries but if you want to ensure an early crop, before the main fruiting season starts, the sooner you take the necessary steps the better.

For those without a greenhouse, cloches are the answer. And for this job I prefer glass as I believe it gives results some days earlier than polythene. If you have several rows of plants pick the strongest growing one to put the cloches over. For the moment, clear the row of weeds, dead leaves, etc., and loosen the surrounding soil, leaving all nice and clean.

Spray with captan once and repeat this at fortnightly intervals, after the cloches have been placed in position, when flowering starts. Don't put the cloches on until the middle of February—the very cold weather beforehand will have a beneficial effect on the plants' subsequent efforts, strange as that may seem to some people.

It will be necessary to do some hand pollinating, that is, transferring pollen from one flower to another, so as to avoid mis-shapen fruit. This is easily done with a small brush (from Johnny's paint-box, perhaps) as shown in inset A. If you haven't a brush, use a piece of cotton-wool. This really ought to be done every day.

If you have a greenhouse, cold or warm, you can do even better. At the end of the month pot up promising-looking plants—one to a 9 in. pot—in good compost, either soil-less or John Innes. Put them on the staging and treat as described above, plus extra care to ensure that the soil in the pots never dries out.

When the fruit has started setting you'll probably find that the plants need watering every day—and give them liquid manure or fertiliser added to the water once a week to ensure getting really plump fruit. Each pot ought to produce, on average, about a pound and look something like inset B.

These plants should never be forced a second time. They need not be thrown away but can be returned to the garden to grow naturally next year. They will probably provide you with early runners for rooting.

GLOXINIAS

In my opinion, the Gloxinia is one of the finest flowering pot plants the amateur can raise in a greenhouse without any difficulty provided he can maintain a temperature of 60°F. (16°C.).

Some specialist growers start the tubers off in boxes or 3 in. pots of equal parts of peat and sand, just nicely moist, but I think the average gardener can save himself the work of potting on by starting each tuber in a 6 in. pot. In this case use a compost such as John Innes No. 2, making sure the pots are well crocked, unless you are using plastic pots, to ensure good drainage.

If you wish to make up your own compost use equal parts of good loam, peat or leaf-mould and well-decayed manure. Add enough sand to make the whole mixture sufficiently porous so that it drains well. This drainage question is very important. For that reason the compost must be made nicely moist before the tubers are pressed into the surface of it, leaving the top of each tuber exposed.

At this stage only a little water is given, without wetting the tubers, until it is obvious that they are growing well. After this point is reached there is much less likelihood of the tubers rotting, but you should keep water off the leaves from now on.

As soon as buds appear, add a liquid fertiliser to the water once a week and keep the plants shaded from direct sunshine. A lower temperature of 55°F. is sufficient from now on. Stand near the glass and keep shaded.

There is a wide choice of named varieties available in self-coloured form; pink, blue and scarlet in one such as Satin Beauty, shown in inset A, as well as many with edges of shades different from the base colour, such as Princess Mary (red and white) shown in inset B.

You may think tubers rather expensive but remember that these tubers will last for several years.

You can, if you wish, grow them from seed. Sown now, they should be in bloom from late summer onwards. Seed needs 65° to 70°F. for germination. When about one inch high, pot the seedlings up singly and grow as explained above.

TOMATO GROWING

Those people with a heated greenhouse can now make a start with tomatoes. Those sown this month are intended for early crops in the greenhouse. For a later supply in the house and for growing out-of-doors, the seed need not be sown until March.

For sowing, you need a good seed compost. I prefer the soilless ones as they seem able to make a really good root system in such a light-textured medium and this is very important in the production of robust plants.

Place the seed singly, an inch apart, on the surface of the compost and then push each seed into it about $\frac{1}{4}$ in. deep, with the blunt end of a pencil.

You need a constant temperature of 60°F. (16°C.) at night, a little higher during the day will not matter.

To avoid having to heat the whole house to this temperature, place the seed-box, covered with glass and paper, in a propagating frame, so that only the frame need be heated to this figure. The seed should germinate in a week, when the paper should be removed. A week later remove the glass as well.

When the seedlings are large enough to handle (by the leaf, not the stem, as in inset B), when they will be about 2 in. high, pot up each one separately. Grow them on in these pots, whether they are to be planted outside or inside, until the first truss of fruit has set.

If you have them, it is a good plan to use peat pots for this purpose as then the whole thing can be planted out, thus avoiding any root disturbance in the process. This is quite important as we, of course, wish them to reach maturity as quickly as possible.

Once the seedlings have been potted, the pots must be stood on the greenhouse staging close to the glass and light so that they do not become leggy. Short, sturdy plants are best.

They should be watered regularly and thus kept moist, but must not be saturated. Use water kept in the greenhouse so that its temperature has been raised. Water out of the mains is too cold.

BULBS IN BOWLS

At this time of year quite a number of people are disappointed because the bulbs they have been raising in bowls of fibre have not yet flowered or have not grown as much as they had hoped. To diagnose the cause of a particular failure is not really possible unless one knows all the details of their treatment to date. But it may be helpful to give the causes of some common problems and to suggest some remedies.

Watering is probably the basis of more problems than anything else. The fibre should be kept nicely moist *at all times*. Bowls of bulbs tend to be forgotten until the fibre has dried out and they are then given a good soaking. This is quite wrong. A bowl of fibre needs watering as soon as it gives a hollow ring when tapped. And when it is watered tip it up so that all excess moisture runs out. Done carefully, the bulbs won't fall out. In any case, you can hold them in by placing the fingers of one hand between them. Over-watering may cause the leaf tips to turn yellow or the base of the bulb and the roots to rot away. On the other hand, lack of water is often the cause of daffodil buds dying before opening.

When hyacinth leaves grow up far above a stunted bloom as in inset A the cause is usually too much warmth, or the bringing of the bowl into the warmth too soon. This is difficult to correct once it has occurred but the remedy most likely to succeed is to water the bowl twice, at weekly intervals, with $\frac{1}{4}$ of a teaspoonful of sulphate of ammonia dissolved in a pint of water and to cover the whole surface of the fibre with damp moss. If the flower has started to open low down use potash instead of ammonia in the water.

When one bulb in a bowl has not developed as much as the others it may be possible to correct this by placing over it a small flower-pot, see inset B. Remove this regularly to see what progress is being made.

The growers of the bulbs specially prepared for flowering at Christmas or early in the year mostly provide an instruction leaflet with the bulbs and it cannot be over-emphasised how important it is to read this and to follow it exactly throughout the growing period. If you are not prepared to do this, you are really wasting your money buying the bulbs.

VINES

The growing of grape-vines both indoors and out is increasing rapidly nowadays due to the upsurge in popularity of wine-making at home.

If you intend to have a go, now is the time to do something about it. Order your vine, perferably in a pot, so that you can stand it in the greenhouse until it shows signs of new growth, probably the end of February or early March. That is the time to put it in its permanent position.

Care must be taken to see that the site is suitable. If you have medium garden soil that drains reasonably well you are lucky. That will suit the vine splendidly. If you have clay, really heavy soil or very light stuff, this will have to be dug out of a hole about a yard square and replaced with a suitable mixture. Ideally, this should consist of loam, 5 parts, decayed manure or compost 1 part, plus 1 further part of mortar rubble to improve the drainage. If you have on hand any wood ash, potash or bone-meal or bone-flour add some of that, too, to the mixture.

You can plant the vine outside the house to grow up against a south-facing wall if you wish. Better still, plant it outside a cool greenhouse or conservatory to take the main stem inside, as shown. Wrap the stem in straw and sacking where it goes through the wall. Stuff further sacking in the gap to fill the space.

Before planting, break up the ball of soil that comes out of the pot carefully with your hands so that you can spread out the roots to their full extent. Keep them in that position in the hole by filtering fine soil over them and pressing down. Make sure the roots are nicely moist at all times until the plant is well-established, when it will become quite hardy.

After planting, give it a mulch of rotted manure or compost. The main stem inside the greenhouse should be cut back immediately above the first bud above the staging pointing in the direction in which you want to train the vine. Normally, one cultivates one or two main rods for the bearing of fruit—one bunch per 9 in. of rod, according to the text-book, but that, I assure you, calls for a great deal of will-power!

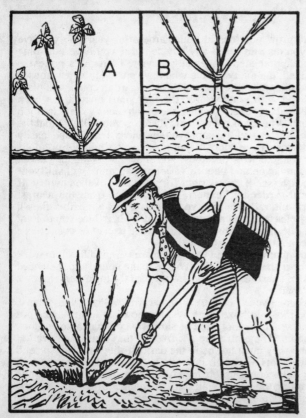

CURRANTS

Once the bushes are established, currants (black, in particular, as well as red and white) are a really worth-while crop—provided you can keep the birds off the fruit. These bushes can be planted now, or as soon as the soil is in a suitable condition.

If your soil is on the light side, it will suit red and white currants better than black but to stop moisture draining out of it too quickly give a good top dressing of rotted compost every second year.

Where soil is really heavy or has a high proportion of clay, black currants will appreciate its moisture-holding quality but at the same time its general texture should be improved. This is best achieved by deep digging. Take out the top spit and throw it on one side. Dig over the second spit, working into it a generous helping of long strawy manure or well-rotted compost and all the bonfire ash you have on hand. Return the top-soil, except where the bushes are to stand. This part of the top-soil can be replaced as you plant. The bushes need to stand 4 to 5 ft. apart and three inches of soil above the roots is quite sufficient. Pack fine soil around the roots and tread firm as you do so. Firm planting is essential but you do not want to make the surface one solid cake of mud. The planted bush is shown in inset B.

In inset A we show how such a bush should be pruned immediately after planting. Each branch is cut back to about 6 in. of the soil, so as to form a strong base framework on which the bush can subsequently develop. The object is to encourage the bush to make new wood as it is the wood produced one summer that fruits the next. All wood that has fruited is removed each year, after the fruit has been picked, to continue the encouragement of new wood formation. To this end, you will find that they respond very well to generous feeding. It is also wise to apply a nitrogen fertiliser once a year.

The pruning of red and white currants is rather different. In winter, shorten all leading shoots by about 6 in. and all side-shoots cut back to an inch of the point of origin, to induce the bush to make fruiting spurs. In summer, side-shoots are shortened to about five leaves. Leading shoots are not touched in summer.

15

POTATOES

Do you intend to grow potatoes in your garden this year? If you have done so before you may not need any advice but if you have not some guidance may be appreciated, especially in view of today's prices!

On the other hand, the many people who have moved into new houses where uncultivated land has to be turned into a garden could well plant nearly all their land with potatoes for the first year, once it has been cleared of weeds and dug over, because the potato does a first-class job as a soil cultivator. When you come to dig the crop you will find that the condition of the soil is greatly improved, is more friable and easily worked than you may have thought possible by the humble potato.

So, if you are going to grow potatoes, you should do something about it now. Study a catalogue and choose varieties you think will suit your needs. Now check to see if this is right for your part of the country. If you have no local gardening "expert", seek advice from the nearest allotment or horticultural society. Even if you aren't a member they'll probably be very pleased to help you; they may even induce you to join! In most cases it doesn't cost much more than one packet of cigarettes a year! And the benefits are enormous.

Calculating how many you need for a given area is not difficult to work out if you remember that you get about 6 to 8 to the pound and they need planting about 8 in. apart (earlies) and 15 in. apart for the others, in rows 15 in. or more apart.

When you receive your seed treat it carefully. Place the tubers, "rose" end uppermost, in boxes or trays, as shown in inset A, and put these in a light, airy, frost-proof shed or similarly cool place, to produce short, sturdy shoots. They must not get frozen, they must not have too much warmth and they must not be in the dark. If they are, they'll send out long, spindly shoots as shown in inset B. Starting them into growth early in this way helps considerably in getting an early crop. But don't be tempted into planting too early. Wait until the danger of frost killing the shoots has passed unless you can protect them with straw, etc.

OREGON GRAPE: A BARGAIN FROM THE WILD WEST

AWAY BACK in 1823, when America as an independent country was a mere 47 years old, a British plant collector called David Douglas returned by sea from California with an unusual prickly shrub which looked very much like a dwarf holly.

When it was planted in Britain, it bore purple grapelike fruit with a waxy bluish bloom.

In fact in its native North America it was called the Oregon Grape after the State in which it was first discovered.

For several years after the Oregon Grape's arrival, bushes sold for 10 guineas (£10.50 if you need reminding) a time, so keen were gardeners to get possession of such an exquisitely beautiful and rare shrub.

However, gradually, as word spread around how easy it was to grow the Oregon Grape, the price dropped. Nowadays you can buy a bush for about £1.

The Oregon Grape really is a most attractive plant. In summer its evergreen leaves are a glistening dark green and with the onset of autumn and winter they are tinged with red.

As early as February, but more usually in March and April, the shrub, with its distinctive prickly holly-like leaves, bears sweetly scented clusters of Chartreuse yellow flowers.

After a couple of months or so the flowers fade and give way to the formation of the purple berries which are generally ripe in July and August.

The fruit is useful as well as decorative. It can be used to make delicious jam, jelly or pies in much the same way as you would use a fruit like the blackcurrant.

The original home of the Oregon Grape, lying between the Blue Mountains and the Pacific, and itself almost cut in two by the 12,000ft. Cascade Range, provides an enormous number of climatic and plant life possibilities.

It is the State of fruit (plums, apples, strawberries), farming (wheat, oats, barley), fishing (halibut, oyster, salmon) and forestry. In this last respect not only does Oregon grow a fifth of the United States' timber, but it also provides the Sitka spruce which is the most common commercial conifer in forests in Britain.

And the emblem of bountiful Oregon, rich too in gold, silver, copper and platinum? The Oregon Grape, of course. What a marvellous choice. For it combines a prickly toughness with fruitfulness, so symbolic of man's mighty efforts and huge rewards.

In Britain the Oregon Grape normally grows to between 2ft. and 3ft. tall with a 3ft. spread and it will thrive absolutely anywhere in any kind of garden soil in sun or shade.

In fact the shrub is extremely useful for carpeting the difficult areas of soil around tall trees. You know the sort of spots I mean: positions where the constant dripping from overhanging branches kills the grass and most vegetation underneath, and perhaps, too, the soil is in the shade of tall buildings. Yet another situation where the Oregon Grape grows better than most other shrubs is the sort of site that is blasted by icy winds in winter.

I have devoted an entire small bed to my Oregon Grapes and I have planted the bushes just 2ft. apart so that I have a completely tightly knitted mass of leaves and yellow flowers.

In spring these flowers are really a delight. The numerous dense yellow clusters measure up to 5in. across and look very much like the flowers of the lilac. Even the masses of deep purple, often more a violet black, berries have a certain eye-appeal, nestling among the fresh young foliage.

If planted as a single bush, an Oregon Grape will probably reach 5ft. in time. However, every April I trim my bushes over lightly with the secateurs so that they remain tight and bushy.

The best month to plant new bushes is April. As I mentioned earlier, any kind of soil is suitable and that includes sand and chalk. But a little preparation will work wonders.

I suggest that you fork over your soil and incorporate some peat. The peat improves the soil's texture and enables the newly planted bush to make strong roots.

Normally the leaves will be a dark lustrous green, but in exposed windy positions there will be a tendency for them to take on a scarlet tinge. This does no harm to the bush and many people find it an added attraction.

If you would prefer a variety of the Oregon Grape with rich reddish-purple leaves during winter and early spring, you can grow *Atropurpurea*—or to give the shrub its full botanical tongue-twisting name, *Mahonia aquifolium atropurpureum.*

Once you have an Oregon Grape bush it is a remarkably simple job to increase your stock.

The seed from the berries or the berries themselves can be planted in a sheltered part of the garden in August and by the following April you will have seedling bushes.

Alternatively, you can increase your stock by "cuttings," by using 4in. long tips of the leading shoots. The cuttings should be taken in July, dipped in hormone rooting powder and planted in a shaded, sheltered spot until the following year, by which time they will have taken root.

Actually, if you follow my method of lightly pruning your bushes in April, you will find that the shrubs will make sucker growth at the base which can be removed to form a new bush.

Oregon Grapes need no feeding and they do not suffer from any pest apart from the thrush population who find those exceptionally juicy berries irresistible.

Initially, I gave my bushes a thick mulch of peat to remove the need to do any weeding, and now that they are a dense light-excluding mass, no attention is required.

Rarely will you find a fruit bush which needs so little or no help from you.

And isn't it a wonderful thought that at a time when so much is going up in price that £1 will buy you a bush that more than 150 years ago sold for 10 times that amount?

18

SHALLOTS AND ONION SETS

February signifies the beginning of a new year in the vegetable grower's calendar, as we can now make a start, provided weather and soil are suitable, with shallots, to be followed at the end of the month by onion sets.

No special preparation is needed for shallots provided the ground is in good heart and has been recently cultivated. It must be sufficiently dry to be friable and not so sodden that it is trodden into a solid cake. If your soil is wet like this, wait until it improves. If you can go ahead, rake in a dressing of lime, clearing weeds at the same time.

If your shallots (or onion sets) have pieces of long, dry stalks attached, snip these off (see inset A) before planting. Otherwise the birds seem to love having a tug-of-war until they have uprooted the bulbs.

Just push each bulb into the soil as shown in inset B, leaving only the top third exposed.

Plant them 6 to 9 in. apart in rows 1 ft. apart. A sunny spot is best. Fortunately they seldom suffer from onion-fly and properly ripened and stored they'll last for a year. In fact, save some for planting the following season.

The last few remarks also apply to onion sets. Spacing is similar to that for shallots but push these bulbs just below the surface.

The onions grown from sets are usually rather flatter in shape than those grown from seed but there is now on the market a new type that produces results that are almost as globular as seed-produced ones. These are called All-Rounder, a name that is suitable not only for their shape but also, I understand, to their cropping quality throughout the country.

If, after you have obtained your onion sets, the weather makes it impossible for you to plant them straightway they must be unpacked and laid out in a single layer in a box in full light in a cool, dry place to prevent them shooting before they go into the ground. If this happens, many of them may well be spoilt and their virtue of not "bolting" (running to seed) largely destroyed.

19

EARLY BEANS

Here are some ways in which we can beat the weather and the calendar in producing early bean crops—without actually working in the garden as the ground is so wet—if you have a greenhouse or cold frame.

First of all, broad beans. You may have sown some in the autumn as I suggested but in many parts of the country that sowing may have failed because of the excessively wet weather. If yours have failed sow some more in a box about 4 in. deep. Almost fill it with some good compost such as John Innes No. 1. Sow the seeds in it (as in inset A) 2 in. apart each way and about an inch deep, adding some more compost if necessary to bring the top of it to within one inch of the top of the box.

Place the box in the greenhouse or frame, in which the glass should have been cleaned inside and out to ensure that they get the maximum light available.

Later on, when the plants have grown, you will have to give them adequate ventilation to harden them off before they are planted outside. If the weather is suitable, the boxes could wisely be stood outside in a sheltered spot for a week or two before planting out. These should mature much earlier than those sown *in situ* in the spring.

French beans can be treated in a similar way, only with these they are sown and matured in pots in the greenhouse. You need large pots, about 9 in. ones, and these are almost filled with similar compost. But as these are to be grown completely in the pots John Innes No. 2 would be better than No. 1.

Push three seeds into the compost about one inch deep, spacing them evenly round the pot, as shown in inset B. Assuming the compost is nicely moist, as it should be when you sow the seeds, don't water the seedlings until they show the first pair of true leaves. Later on, the plants will need supporting with twiggy sticks and as soon as flowers form it is as well to syringe them to help the flowers to set, particularly if the atmosphere in your greenhouse is dry. A regular weekly feed with weak liquid manure also helps to ensure getting a reasonable crop. They also need a reasonable supply of *rain*-water, for preference, at all times.

RHUBARB

If you do not grow rhubarb in your garden, now is the time to remedy this omission. It is a very useful crop, as established plants will provide pickings, or perhaps I should say pullings, from February to August from outdoor plants, while some can be forced for use in the kitchen during the winter. This means that you can have rhubarb on the home menu for the greater part of the year.

In order to make the season of use as long as possible you can obtain seed of an early variety such as Glaskins Perpetual, followed by Prince Albert and a late variety such as Victoria. Although growing from seed means a longer wait for a crop, it is, in the long run, the better way as it is not always possible to obtain roots of the varieties you require from local nurseries or shops.

Seed can be sown now, 1 in. deep. Thin out to 6 in. apart and plant in their permanent positions 3 ft. apart next autumn or the following spring.

Prepare the ground well where they are to be planted as they should stay there for four or five years before being lifted, divided and given a new site. Dig about two bucketfuls of well-rotted manure into each hole, leaving the tips of the shoots above ground level. Firm in well with the feet. The plants must be allowed to become fully established and no stalks should be pulled the first year after planting out, except any stalk that is obviously going to produce a flower head. This must be pulled out (as shown in inset) as soon as it is seen, provided it can be removed without uprooting the plant. If there is danger of disturbance, *cut* it off.

When the time comes for pulling your crop, never denude a plant. Always leave at least four good stems in position in order that the plant can produce more roots and leaves and can build up a big crown for the following year.

In the autumn give the plant a generous top-dressing of manure or compost. If you can cover this with straw to a depth of about a foot in December you'll get a really early crop the next year.

BEGONIAS

Tuberous begonias can now be started into growth if you have a greenhouse or other place where you can maintain a temperature of 65°F. (18°C.). The ideal is a propagating frame that can be heated in this way, as few people wish to incur the expense of maintaining such a temperature in the whole of the greenhouse.

An ordinary seed-box will do quite well. Fill it with John Innes compost No. 1 or a mixture of leafmould (or peat) loam and silver sand in equal parts. Water it, and allow to drain thoroughly.

Place the tubers firmly on the compost in the box, 3 or 4 inches apart, according to tuber size; the larger they are, the greater the spacing. Cover them with half an inch of compost from the bag or heap that has not been watered. Some people do not cover them but I believe in doing so, particularly if the tubers are already showing pink growth points, which is a mark in their favour as it shows they have started to move of their own volition and are, therefore, less likely to rot before roots have formed.

Keep the soil between the corms moist and avoid wetting the actual tubers. They like shade and a moist atmosphere.

When growth is about an inch high, pot up each one separately in a 5 in. pot in a slightly richer mixture, such as John Innes No. 2. This is for those that are to go into a cold-frame in mid-May for a fortnight to harden off before being planted in the garden, in a shady spot, in early June.

If you intend to flower them as pot plants in the greenhouse or home, use John Innes No. 3 when you pot them up, to avoid having to move them again.

Our insets show: (A) how the tuber should be planted, concave side uppermost; (B) a variety called Marmorata in which its carmine brilliance is vividly offset with a white marbling effect; (C) a giant double strain called Multiflora Maxima, where the colours range from white, through yellow and orange, to red.

PARSNIPS

On light land or where the soil is in a dry enough condition to be worked into a fine tilth we can make a start with our vegetable seed-sowing. But don't be impatient, wait until the soil is right—even next month is early enough. The first sowing is parsnips, if you like them.

If you want to grow really large ones you need ground that was well manured for a previous crop and dug two spits deep. If this isn't available and you want to manure now, use only well-rotted stuff and get it down into the second spit, otherwise you'll find when you come to dig the parsnips that the roots have divided into several almost useless sections.

If you have stony ground your best plan would be to make holes, as shown in inset A, about 9 in. apart, and 18 in. deep. Into these holes shift fine soil mixed with sand. On the top of this sow 3 seeds in each place and cover with a little fine soil. Later, when the seeds have germinated, remove all but the best one of the three so that it can develop fully on its own.

Where the land is suitable for sowing a row in the normal way, draw a drill about an inch deep, sow and cover over. For more than one row the drills should be at least a foot apart. The seedlings will have to be thinned later to about 9 in. apart, so sow thinly.

Where space is very limited, try sowing a row of lettuce 2 or 3 in. away from the parsnips on each side. The lettuce will germinate and mature much quicker than the parsnips and you'll get two crops for the space of one. The same sort of land suits both.

Most people will not want to grow a long variety such as Exhibition, shown in inset B, unless they want to win a prize at their local flower show, so when you buy your seed, choose a shorter variety, usually called "intermediate", as that will prove very satisfactory in soil that has not been cultivated deeply enough for the long ones.

If you are going to sow the lettuce as well, choose one of the butterhead varieties. With these you can sow again, at intervals, if you wish, until July.

ONIONS

Although the production of onions of a moderate size suitable for use in the kitchen is much easier from sets (small bulbs pushed into the soil like shallots) there are still many people who prefer facing up to the challenge of growing exhibition-size onions from seed sown out of doors next month—a laudable characteristic that made Britain great!

It may surprise some people that the onion is a deep-rooting vegetable. For that reason they need deeply-dug soil, in a sunny position, that has been well-manured in autumn or early winter. Assuming you can give them that, the important thing is to give the ground one dressing of lime now and another a few days before you sow the seed.

This will be nicely worked in when you rake and tread, rake and tread, until the surface soil is a really fine tilth. And it *must* be dry enough to do that before you sow. If it is not, wait until it is—you can still sow in April without much ultimate loss of time.

Sow thinly in drills about a foot apart. Even then you'll still need to thin them out. And do it *early*—to 3 in. apart, even if the thinnings are not large enough to use as "Spring onions" in salads.

When next you thin, to about 9 in. apart, the thinnings will be large enough to use.

Another space-saving idea is to sow radishes in rows between the onions. They germinate and mature quickly and will be pulled for use long before they can be any impediment to the onion crop.

Curiously enough, the radishes are said to deter the onion-fly, as does parsley sown in patches nearby. Another, even more effective deterrent to the fly is to avoid crushing any foliage of the plants you leave in when you are thinning out. The smell of the sap seems to act like a magnet to the fly.

Inset B shows the two forms in which some onions often mature, the oval and the globular shape. Use the oval ones for the kitchen and put the others on the show bench if you are an exhibitor.

A popular variety for growing in this way is Ailsa Craig, which can be sown again in August to provide a crop for use the following summer.

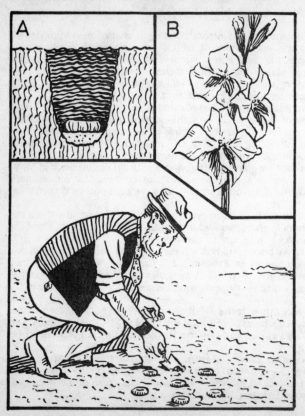

GLADIOLI

From now on, as soon as the soil is in a workable condition, we can start putting in gladioli. Plant a number each fortnight until the end of April and you should have a splendid display of bloom from July to September, provided you have chosen varieties covering the three periods, early, mid and late, or as shown in some catalogues, 1, 2, and 3.

Any good medium soil is suitable, provided it has been well worked and manured. The only difference that need be made is that in lighter soil the corms should be planted about 5 in. deep instead of 4 in., as is usual on heavier ground.

Set them in groups of 5 or 6 in circles, squares or any designs you like planned to a certain shape to fill given spaces. The corms should be put in with a trowel, about 6 in. apart.

If the ground seems to be on the wet side, which also means it may be rather cold to encourage growth, place a handful of sand at the bottom of each hole, to improve drainage, in order to prevent the corm rotting before it starts to grow. In extreme cases, of course, it would be better to defer planting until later, when the soil has dried out more.

They produce splendid, large spikes of flowers for cutting but will need a supporting cane for each spike, and when you cut them, cut through the stem alone, not through the leaves. Cutting the leaves is detrimental to the formation of the corm for next season.

Many of the ladies nowadays prefer the smaller, more delicate spikes of the so-called Butterfly and Nanus types for their flower arrangements. One of the newest of this type is shown in Inset B. Called Coronado, it comes in about ten different shades of colour. These rather smaller corms usually produce two or three spikes of flowers each and in most areas do not require supports. They also flower about a week earlier than the Butterfly ones.

25

A NEW BEAN

We are all accustomed to the introduction each year of new varieties of vegetables, flowers, etc., many of which are well worth growing.

Now we have not merely a new *variety* but a new *vegetable*. This is a rather sweeping claim that I find rather hard to swallow—if the producers will forgive that word. It is, in fact, a relative of the Soya Bean, but do not be put off by that fact.

This new bean has a splendid flavour and is so rich in nutriment that it is claimed to be of more value to mankind than meat, bread or milk!

But first, of course, we have to grow it. Its name is Fiskeby V.

Early next month is the time to start if you can provide some warmth in greenhouse or home. Sow the seeds singly in peat pots for preference as each one can then be planted out of doors without disturbance in May, but harden them off in a cold-frame first, of course. Use an ordinary seed-box for sowing the seed if you do not have peat pots or do not want to buy them.

If you cannot start them off in heat, wait until May and sow them out of doors. Put them in short rows, side by side, about 9 in. apart. Plant the seeds 1½ in. deep, 3 in. apart in the row.

They aren't fussy about soil but will naturally do better in ground that is in good shape. And as an experiment, I think they deserve as good a situation as you can give them. They are quite hardy and do not appear to be affected by any disease or pest, which is certainly an advantage to the grower.

Although it has come to us from the Chinese who in their warmer climate have grown a bean of this kind for 5,000 years, this particular one has been bred and raised in Scotland further north than Aberdeen for over 10 years.

The crop should be harvested from August to October. It can be eaten green (boiled for 3-4 minutes) or can be left to ripen on the vine when it can be stored for use all through the winter. The fresh green beans can also go into your freezer, if you have one.

DAHLIAS

If you wish to increase your stock of dahlias you should soon start the tubers stored for the winter into growth again. This is done in the greenhouse or heated frame. They need a temperature of 55° to 60°F. (12° to 15°C.) really, but you can still do it if you maintain a temperature of only 45°F in your greenhouse, but they will not develop so quickly. To save heating the whole house to 60°F, use a propagator.

Inspect your tubers, remove any mildew there may be on them and cut off any tuber that has rotted. Dust any parts thus affected with flowers of sulphur. Then pack the tubers on a bed of peat and sand in equal parts in a deepish box and cover them, up to the base of the stems, with more peat and sand. Make the mixture nicely moist and keep it that way but don't overdo it until they have started growing.

Once you can see that the eyes (buds) have started growing, you can either leave them to develop into shoots sufficiently long (about 3 in.) to use as cuttings or you can divide the crowns up into portions each having a tuber and a developing eye. These portions are potted up singly in a mixture of equal parts of good loam, peat and sand and grown on to make nice sturdy plants ready to go out into the garden in early June, after being hardened off.

If you prefer to raise new plants from cuttings, carefully remove each one with a very sharp knife or razor blade, as shown in inset A. Remove all but the top leaves and growing point. Cut the base clearly across just below a leaf joint, dip in water and hormone rooting powder and insert in a pot. Fill the pot with the same mixture as for the crown divisions. Make a hole with a pencil, for example, and insert as shown in inset B. Put in as many cuttings round the edge as the pot will take without the leaves touching. Make them nicely firm, water reasonably well and place in a propagator or greenhouse.

They should be shaded from bright sunlight until rooted, usually about 4 weeks. After that they can come out into a greenhouse or garden frame (after being potted up singly, of course) that is not heated beyond the point of being frost-free.

JAPANESE QUINCE—MAKE A DULL WALL SPARKLE

WHAT DO the months ahead hold for you in the garden? Can you look forward with a gleam of delight in your eye to some really pleasant events? Does spring promise bounteous blossom? Summer, scent and cool green foliage? Autumn, fruit?

Let me draw your attention to a shrub which lives up to the greatest expectations. It is called the Japanese quince and it is a sure winner in all respects for yours, mine, or any garden.

For it is extremely tough: it will grow in any soil and in any situation.

And even if neglected, it will be clothed in gorgeous bloom from as early as February until May. The dark green glossy foliage is lovely too. Then there are lots of fragrant, apple-shaped, greenish yellow fruits in autumn—the quinces.

Japanese quinces cannot be eaten raw. But they do make a superb quince marmalade and quince jelly.

You can also use the fruit to make quince compôte and to add to apples to make quince and apple pie or quince and apple jelly.

I don't know what it is about the quince, but when allied to apples in a pie, the resulting flavour is magnificent.

The Japanese quince is known to some people by different names. Some call it japonica; other folk prefer cydonia.

But in fact, nowadays, cydonia is the botanical name reserved for the European quince, which is a large tree, while the "Japanese" quince is a bush, measuring on average 5ft. by 5ft. when full grown.

There are few shrubs more worthy of a place in your garden than the quince, especially if you allow it to snuggle up to a house wall.

Imagine, if your house is of cold grey stone, like so many houses in Wales, Scotland and the North of England, what a warm, heartening sight it would be to glimpse the flash of the crimson flowers of a quince in spring.

Perhaps your house is of good old English red brick. Then you could choose a variety with sparkling white flowers or glowing pink.

But on the other hand if you are one of the lucky ones with a whitewashed cottage or light-coloured walls to your home, then you have really struck gold.

For against such a background, the quinces are outstanding and can be seen in their full splendour with colourful clusters of flowers up to 2in. in diameter in spring and yellow fruit in autumn.

Rowallane is, in my view, the best and brightest of the reds and it is splendid for cheering up a dull, cold wall, whether it faces north, east, south or west.

Other reds which take my fancy are Knaphill Radiance, with exceptionally large flowers, Crimson and Gold, rather special because its flowers are a regal red with yellow centres, Etna, with large flowers which are borne on a small compact shrub and Spitfire, upright in growth and with flowers of a deep crimson.

And ideal for under a downstairs window is the red-flowered quince called Simonii. It has a height of 3ft. and spread of 5ft. In spring the flowers practically conceal its silvery pendulous branches.

Or what about some flowers in brilliant orange? The variety that you want could well be Boule de Feu, excellent as a wall shrub, or in the open among other garden plants, and especially noted for its abundance of fruit.

In addition there is Knaphill Scarlet—also good incidentally under a window—which, despite its name, produces flowers salmon on the outside and terra cotta inside so that in bright sunlight one has the impression of a mass of fiery orange.

Perhaps I can interest you in some salmon-coloured flowers . . . what about Umbilicata which in time will grow to a large shrub 10ft. tall with a 6ft. spread? Or would you prefer Falconet Charlot, a shrub of similar size and double flowers like little rosettes?

Against the traditional redbrick house the white flowers of Nivalis or Snow are seen to greatest advantage. Even Nature herself seems to have appreciated that white flowers need a darker foil. For both these varieties have branches which are gunmetal coloured instead of the more usual silver.

Finally there is pink Rosea Plena, with double flowers, and Pink Lady: both have clear rose pink flowers while those of Hever Castle are a distinct shrimp pink.

Your chosen quince is best bought "container-grown" from a local nursery and it should be planted between November and March.

Although any ordinary garden soil is suitable, it is well worth while taking the trouble to fork over the planting position beforehand so that the soil has that crumbly texture, so pleasing to the eyes of us gardeners (some added peat might do the trick here), to ensure that the quince is able to form new roots rapidly and become properly established before it is expected to withstand summer droughts.

When planted against a wall, the quince's branches are generally sufficiently rigid to manage without supporting wires.

However, you can help by pruning the shrub annually after flowering in May to keep its proportions right. Your aim should be to train the shrub to a flat fan shape by cutting away the branches which project outwards from the wall.

If grown in the open as a bush, little pruning is required, except to thin out crowded branches after flowering. When selecting the branches to cut back, choose the previous season's growth and reduce in length to two or three buds. Such annual treatment will produce better flowers and fruit.

There are no pests or diseases to worry about and, as the bushes are all self-fertile, you can be certain of a crop of fruit this autumn and every other autumn.

If quince can do wonders for stewed apples in a pie, you will positively marvel at the effect of the bush on a previously dull wall.

Perhaps this is the magic ingredient that your garden has been looking for?

PEAS

March is the month to start your pea growing programme.

The soil must be dry enough to allow you to take out a flat drill about an inch deep in which you sow the seeds 3 in. apart, putting 2 or 3 rows of seeds in each drill. The drills should be as far apart as the final height of the variety, which is usually stated in catalogues (24 in. apart for 24 in. in height, and so on).

Now for some suggested varieties. If you choose Kelvedon Wonder, for example, as a first early pea you can sow this variety again in June to provide an autumn crop. Moreover, this is a good variety for freezing so that you can pop the crop into your freezer for use in winter if you have plenty of other vegetables to use at the time it matures.

As a second early or maincrop pea Hurst Green Shaft is good. Pod length is very good—up to $4\frac{1}{2}$ in., containing as many as eleven peas. It grows to a height of 28 in. but bears its pods only in the top 10 to 12 in. so is easy to pick without backache!

The triple-podded pea, Recette, now has a maincrop partner called Trio which, despite its name, often produces 4 and 5 pods. It has the advantage of maintaining its flavour over a long cropping period, bears a remarkably heavy crop and is good for freezing (inset A).

One of the best ideas I have seen for a long time is the offer of packets of Garden Peas mixed. This gives you a number of varieties (18 to 30 in. high) in one packet. Thus they do not all mature at the same time so that a sowing in mid-March, say, and another in mid-May could well provide your family with all the peas you need from mid-June to the end of September.

Apart from these, what one might call ordinary varieties, have you tried the sugar pea, such as Dwarf de Grace (inset B) or the Asparagus Pea? With these, you cook and eat the whole thing, pod and all. D de G is sown from March to June and must be gathered before the peas enlarge the pod. The Asparagus Pea (sown in April and May) needs no staking and the pods should be picked when they are an inch long—later they may be stringy.

VEGETABLE NURSERY

As we all want to achieve maximum vegetable production from our gardens nowadays we must use our space as economically as possible. For this reason, it is wise to devote one corner to a vegetable nursery. It must be in a good position where it gets maximum sunshine, is not overshadowed by trees, etc., and the soil must be of a kind that will break down into a fine tilth. If it is needed to achieve this, give the ground a heavy dressing of peat and rake it in. Don't do this until the soil is dry enough to be nicely workable when raked. And don't rake deeply. If the soil has not settled down properly after digging tread it into a firm surface and rake it again.

For crops of the cabbage family, Brussels sprouts, etc., sprinkle calomel dust over the surface, 1½ oz. per square yard, and rake it in. This is a good preventive measure against club root. If you know from past experience that your soil is free of club root, there is no need to do this; but if you are in any doubt, use this method of making sure you will have no trouble of this kind.

The vegetables to treat in this way are all those which benefit from being transplanted, such as cabbage, sprouts, broccoli, leeks and kale. The benefit of having them all in one area saves space for other crops, such as all the roots, like carrots and beet, which are not transplanted.

Make shallow drills, not more than one inch deep, 6 in. apart and sow the seeds thinly, so that you do not need to do too much thinning out. Cover lightly and press firm with the back of a rake or a light foot. Later on, of course, you will have to thin the seedlings out to about 3 in. apart so that each develops into a robust, sturdy plant before being transplanted. If the seedlings are crowded they will become tall and spindly.

If you can spare the room I advise you to be a little more venturesome this year and to try some vegetables you may have not grown before. Two are shown in the insets. "A" is a dwarf curled Kale, particularly useful in colder districts, while "B" is kohlrabi, the turnip-rooted cabbage, which does well in dry soil conditions and can be recommended to those who have difficulty in growing turnips well.

LETTUCES

In the south it should now be possible to make a start with the sowing of lettuces out-of-doors, depending on the weather and the condition of your soil. In the north, you may well have to wait until April. Even in the south if the surface of your ground is too wet to rake into a fine tilth wait until its condition is suitable as you will achieve nothing by putting seed into cold inhospitable soil.

One way of overcoming this problem is to put a row of cloches over the area in which you intend to sow to warm and dry that soil. Just two weeks of cloche protection in favourable weather can make an enormous difference.

As soon as you can, draw a drill, only half an inch deep, on land that was dug and manured in the autumn preferably. Sow thinly and as soon as the seedlings are large enough thin out by lifting the seedlings not required in the original row and planting them out (1 ft. apart) in a new row. These should mature about two weeks after those not disturbed. If you continue in this way, sowing and transplanting, throughout the season you should have an adequate supply for a major part of the year.

By the way, if you are growing potatoes this year it is a good, ground-saving plan to grow your lettuce between the potato rows, because the lettuces will mature long before the potatoes.

For successful lettuce growing, in addition to suitably enriched soil, the principal need is to keep the plants always adequately supplied with water. Good drainage is important but at the same time the ground must be capable of retaining enough moisture, as if they receive any check to growth through lacking water they very seldom recover and you get a poor crop.

Inset B shows a cabbage lettuce, Unrivalled, which I find very successful. I also favour Little Gem, a dwarf cos type.

To fill in any gaps in supplies for the kitchen during the salad season, try a variety called Salad Bowl. This lettuce does not produce hearts and you do not cut the whole plant for use. You just pick leaves as and when required.

RUNNER BEANS

I don't think anyone with a suitable piece of land needs persuading to grow runner beans nowadays—particularly since the deep freeze has become so popular.

If, as I hope, you prepared a trench for them in the autumn by digging manure or compost into the second spit and leaving the top rough in a mound along the row, you could wisely now, if the ground is dry enough, lightly rake the top over to help it dry out and warm up. It is not needed yet for the plants or seed as runners are very susceptible to frost. But you could sow a row of radishes on it as they will mature before you need it for the beans. And thin those radishes out early or you'll get all tops and no bottoms!

Don't sow your runners out-of-doors before mid-May, 2 in. deep and about 12 in. apart. If you have cloches, the seed could go in in April.

Otherwise, to produce early plants, sow the seed now, in boxes that are 3 or 4 inches deep. Use some good compost and push the seeds in an inch deep, 3 in. apart each way. Keep the boxes on a shelf close to a window in a shed where the light is good or in a greenhouse close up to the glass so that they do not get "leggy".

The plants should not go out into the garden before the end of May or as soon as you feel all danger of frost has passed, unless you can protect them with cloches. If you start them off in the greenhouse, they should go into a cold frame for about three weeks before going out into the garden.

Runner beans do not necessarily have to be grown up supports, although most people believe they get a better crop that way—and picking is less back-aching! But they can be grown as what we call ground beans. In this case one has to pick out the tops of the climbing shoots to make the beans branch into bushy plants.

One variety, called Sunset, which happens to have pale pink flowers instead of red ones, is a good one to choose for this purpose as it seems to do equally well whether supported or not. You might even grow a row each way and compare results for yourself.

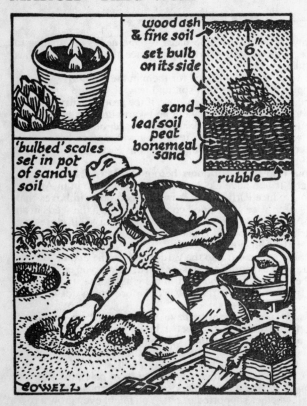

wood ash & fine soil

set bulb on its side

6"

sand

leafsoil
peat
bonemeal
sand

rubble

'bulbed' scales set in pot of sandy soil

COWELL

LILIES

Most lilies, which can be planted out-of-doors now, prefer a partially shaded position, with their feet in the shade, heads in the sun.

At the bottom of the planting holes, which should be wide enough to take groups of four or five bulbs, place a layer of rubble. Fork in plenty of compost made up as shown.

If any of the bulbs are found to be diseased, dust them with sulphur. If blotched marks are seen remove the affected scales and soak the bulbs in a one per cent solution of salicylic acid.

Embed the bulbs in a layer of sand. The depth of planting varies between 4 and 6 in., allowing up to 8 in. for stem-rooting kinds, or twice their widest diameter. Lay them on their sides to prevent moisture collecting among the scales and so causing decay.

Lilies can be increased at this time of year by means of the scales on the bulbs. On some of these you may see miniature bulbs.

Take these scales off and plant them upright in pots of fine sandy soil. They will eventually develop into full-sized flowering bulbs.

If you have a part of the garden devoted to flowering shrubs, plant groups of lilies between the other subjects. If the site happens to be a sloping one, on a bank, for instance, so much the better, as lilies, even the so-called "bog-lilies", do not like ground that is sodden. Drainage is the key-note to success.

There is a very wide choice of varieties, from those 10 ft. tall to others tiny enough for the rock garden, many gloriously scented.

Apart from drainage, which means the plentiful use of sand at planting time, use if you can some well-rotted cow manure. This is good for all lilies but particularly for those called "stem-rooting". These produce roots from the stem *above* the bulb as well as roots below the bulb in the normal way.

Do not be disappointed if your new lilies do not produce many blooms the first season. This quite often happens. They will improve in future years, especially if you cut down all the stems to ground level, after flowering, in the autumn and top dress with cow manure.

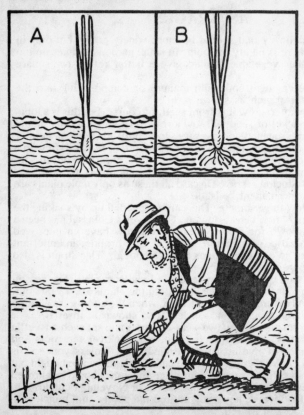

ONIONS

Those who have raised their own seedling onions can now set them out in their maturing positions as soon as the soil is dry enough to work into fine particles. This applies especially to those who sowed their seed in the open last August. Those who raised the seedlings in warmth by sowing in January or February must harden the seedlings off in a cold frame before transplanting. They should be set 6 in. apart in rows 1 ft. apart or slightly more each way if you have the room.

The most important point to watch when planting is the placing of the small bulbs. They must sit on or slightly in the surface soil, as shown in inset B. They must not be planted deeper (certainly NOT as in inset A). If they are they are likely to produce thick-necked onions which seldom keep very well. Handle the little plants with care, so as not to crush the fragile stems, as the resultant odour seems to be extraordinarily alluring to the onion-fly. Plant firmly, pressing the soil around each bulb, but keep the surface of the soil between the rows loose.

If you do not have seedlings available, seed can now be sown in drills 1 in. deep 1 ft. apart. The bed should be firm but have a fine tilth on the surface and, ideally, will have been dug and manured in the autumn.

When the plants from seedlings or seeds are growing well regular dusting with old soot or bonfire ash will be beneficial. And a sprinkling of nitrate of soda or sulphate of ammonia will stimulate growth. Strong growth does not seem to have the same appeal for the onion-fly as the more weakly kind.

If you know you are pestered by this fly, grow your onions from sets (tiny bulbs raised from seed sown last summer). They seem to be much more resistant to it.

Plant the sets $2\frac{1}{2}$ in. deep, 6 in. apart in drills 1 ft. apart, or rather more if you can spare the space. Subsequent care is the same as for seedlings. Some may run to seed but this is often caused by planting too shallowly—in contrast to the planting of young seedlings.

When weeding onions, pull the weeds out by the hand as hoeing often loosens the soil too much, to the detriment of the onion plants.

ASPARAGUS

Asparagus is a delicacy that should be more widely grown but only in gardens where there is plenty of room. In small gardens it takes up too much space—other vegetables would give a better return per square yard.

Asparagus prefers light soil, with manure or compost dug into the second spit of the trench as shown.

The cheapest way to grow it is from seed, of course, but this is a long-term policy. A packet of seed will sow a row 20 ft. long and this should produce the plants needed, on average, to supply the typical family.

You can sow during the latter half of this month or in April. Sow in a drill 1 in. deep, drills being 1 ft. apart if more than one. Thin out to 3 in. apart later and let it stand until you can tell whether any of the seedlings are female by producing berries. Discard all these as only male plants are required for the permanent beds.

The seed is slow to germinate. This can be speeded up by soaking the seed in water for 24 hrs. before sowing. Connover's Colossal has been a variety widely grown for many years but we now have an improved variety, called Martha Washington, which is very prolific, an important consideration, as no one ever seems to have enough. This strain is also resistant to Asparagus Rust.

I said earlier that growing from seed is a long-term plan. The reason for this is that no cutting should be done until the plants are 4 years old. Even then cut only from April to mid-June, when the shoots are about 3 in. high. Cut about 4 in. below soil level, as shown in inset B.

If you grow from plants, buy two-year-old roots and set each on a little mound, see inset A, in the trench 12 in. apart. Cover the roots and sprinkle a dressing of hydrated lime around them, unless your soil is already limy. For an earlier crop, three-year-old plants can be bought but are more expensive. Shoots developing after mid-June should be allowed to mature. When these turn yellow in October or November cut down to ground level. Hand weed, never dig around the plants, and mulch with manure or compost in March.

SOWING ROOT CROPS

In most areas, particularly the south, a start can soon be made with the sowing of root crops, such as carrots, beetroot and turnips.

As a general rule, such crops prefer light, rich soil that has been deeply dug and was manured for a previous crop. Get as near that ideal as you can but do not dig in manure now. There is no reason why you should not work in plenty of sand, peat, bonfire-ash, etc., in order to lighten the soil, if necessary. Work the top when dry enough into a fine tilth by repeatedly treading and raking, at the same time adding a dressing of a compound fertiliser, such as Growmore, in land that has not been manured.

Sow in shallow drills about 15 in. apart. A broom-handle pressed into the soil makes a very suitable depression for this purpose. Sow thinly because they all must be thinned later on to about 6 in. apart. Don't sow too many at any one time. Save some of the seed in your packet to sow about 3 weeks later or make successional sowings until about mid-summer.

There are, of course, many good varieties in most catalogues but our insets show three which have special qualities to recommend them. "A" is a carrot called Sweetheart, a new strain, very early maturing, having only a small core and a very deep colour. Excellent flavour and very good for deep-freezing. "B" is a beetroot called Boltardy. This name is derived from the fact that this beetroot has exceptionally high resistance to "bolting" (running to seed) and can, therefore, be sown very early. It is a deep red throughout, has fine, ringless texture and very good flavour. Have you ever tried using beetroot cooked as a hot vegetable, pulled when about the size of a golf-ball? Their flavour then is better than when used cold in a salad.

Our third inset shows the turnip, Early White Snowball, which as its name indicates is one for early sowing. Its splendid shape, sweet and tender flesh make this one very popular with exhibitors.

If you like radishes in your salads sow some between the rows of the other root crops.

HARDY ANNUALS

Between now and early May is the period for sowing hardy annuals.

They should have good, rich soil which does not dry out too quickly in summer as they need to be moist at all times to ensure that they grow quickly and continuously as they must complete their growth in a comparatively short time for you to obtain a fine floral display.

They can, of course, be given a bed to themselves, sowing in bold, irregular patches, to give a patch-work quilt effect, that is really well worthwhile. Many people, however, find these annuals very useful for filling in odd patches in other borders and they look very effective in such situations. Don't forget to pay attention to the heights of the different kinds as you don't want short ones hidden by taller neighbours.

Those with large seeds, such as Nasturtiums, can be sown singly, at least a foot apart, as this will avoid the necessity for thinning later on. Push each seed in with a finger, an inch deep. Nasturtiums, by the way, are an exception to the general rule in that they flower better, producing less leaf, when grown in poor, sandy soil.

The fine-seeded ones, like Clarkia and Godetia, should be sown broadcast, as thinly as you can. They barely need covering and will have to be thinned out later. Do it after a shower, if you can, as it is then much easier.

There is a splendid assortment of such flowers in most catalogues, but the insets show two you may not have grown. "A" is Bartonia (also called Mentzelia) which comes from California. It grows about 1½ ft. high, produces masses of very showy flowers—golden yellow in what is probably the best variety, called Aurea. This one will grow almost anywhere.

The second inset shows Cacalia or Tassel Flower which surprisingly few people seem to know. It is easily grown, is very useful for cutting as it is most attractive in bouquets or for table decoration. The variety recommended, Coccinea, is bright orange-scarlet, same height as Bartonia, and, as you can see in the drawing, the flowers clearly show why it is likened to a tassel.

BERBERIS—A SHRUB FOR ANY GARDEN

SOME PLANTS are born lucky: from the very outset everything goes well for them. Others, however, have to struggle hard all their lives to achieve any success at all.

That very large shrub family called berberis most certainly comes into the first category.

If ever there was a shrub that was everything to all gardeners, this must surely be it.

Firstly, the family consists of some 450 different species, some of which are evergreen and others which lose their leaves in winter.

Secondly, with few exceptions, these shrubs will grow anywhere, in any kind of soil, including shallow, thin soils which will support little else.

Thirdly, they produce the sort of abundance of pretty flowers that make visitors to the garden exclaim: "That's nice. What do you call that?"

Many bushes also produce magnificent autumn displays of coloured leaves.

But, best of all are the berries. In autumn these can be coral coloured, scarlet, blue, purple, or black and they can add a real touch of magic to an otherwise dull spot in the garden right into winter.

You could also regard these berries as something of a bonus. Certainly you would not go out into the garden and eat them straight from the bush. But you could gather them to make a jam with a tart, pleasant flavour, or a delicious jelly. You could use them too to make fruit flans and pies.

You could hardly do better than to make your first choice the variety Buccaneer which soars to 6ft. with a spread of 5ft. It has yellow flowers in May and June which are followed by really large bunches of berries first pearl pink and later turning to brilliant scarlet.

The leaves too turn a fiery scarlet in autumn before dropping off with the lash of winter winds.

Another splendid berberis for scarlet berries is Barbarossa, with a growth habit very similar to its close relative Buccaneer. Most years I expect to see the branches of Barbarossa weighed down with bunches of plump, grapelike berries. Both of these berberises are descended from wild Chinese species.

Yet another berberis from China is gagnepainii. It sounds quite a mouthful, but its name is worth remembering. For this is an extremely useful shrub.

It is evergreen, has yellow flowers, black berries with a blue bloom and grows to about 4ft. It also does well on chalk and makes a superb thick hedge which needs little if any clipping. Didn't I tell you that berberises really and truly offer something for everyone?

Then there is the marvellous evergreen berberis Darwinii, which is called after the famous naturalist Charles Darwin, who discovered the shrub in Chile.

Darwin's berberis, which can grow to 10ft., is one of the

best shrubs you can have in the garden. It is covered in clusters of rich yellow, sometimes orange tinged, flowers in April and May, and these are followed by masses of edible blue berries amid the holly-like leaves.

In the neighbouring Argentine, the 6ft.-high evergreen berberis commonly called Orange King grows wild. It is distinctly beautiful because it produces orange flowers in spring which darken in April to red and later lead to purple berries with a greyish bloom.

But these are mainly tall berberises. What about the gardener who is after something smaller?

First there is the Chinese berberis called candidula. It is a real labour-saving shrub which grows well in shade. When fully grown it is just one and a half feet high with a 3ft. spread. So it is ideal for providing a weed-preventing ground covering around other smaller shrubs.

Candidua is virtually evergreen, with dark green leaves, silvery underneath and bright yellow flowers which lead to oval purple berries in autumn.

I also recommend the berberis called thunbergii. It has a couple of 1½ft. high forms with rich purple red leaves through spring and summer and ovoid scarlet berries in autumn. The one I particularly like is Nana which has orange yellow flowers and is almost thornless.

Other low growing berberises, from 1ft. to 3ft. high, are the dwarf forms of stenophylia called Coccinea, Corallina and Etna. Coccinea has red buds and coral flowers in spring, while Corallina has coral buds and yellow flowers. Etna erupts into a mass of fiery orange blossom in April.

However, do not choose these three if it is berries you are after. You would be far better with some of the ones that I have mentioned previously.

Finally, what about growing the 4ft. high barberry which grows wild in Europe, including Britain? It produces pendulous clusters of bright translucent berries which are suitable for making preserves.

The shrub, called Berberis vulgaris, was once valued by herbalists who used the bark and stems in the preparation of a cure for jaundice.

You can buy a berberis for around £1 and you can plant it any time if you buy it container-grown. There is little you have to do in the way of preparing the soil except to fork it over lightly.

But let me give you a few tips to be absolutely sure of success.

Berberises which lose their leaves can be planted in full sun or partial shade; evergreen kinds are best in partial or full shade.

If you collect a bush from the nursery, choose one which is no more than 18in. high. You will find that it will transplant more easily than a larger, older shrub.

If you are planting a hedge, the shrubs should be spaced 2ft. apart and the topmost branches trimmed back very slightly to encourage the formation of bushy growth.

Pruning is generally not required, but if you must, deciduous types should be pruned in February and evergreen kinds after flowering.

For colour, fruit, versatility and general ease of cultivation the berberis is indeed hard to beat. Why not try one in your garden and see if you agree with me?

MULCHING

Although at the moment of writing, my own ground is, to put it mildly, too wet, I am a great believer in the maxim that Nature has a wonderful way of restoring the balance. In other words, it will not be long before we are complaining about the lack of rain, I am sure.

It is, therefore, wise to try to make the best of both worlds. This we can do by mulching. And the mulching must be done while the ground is still wet. If we put on a mulch once the ground has dried out we do more harm than good.

What should we use? The best material, of course, is manure, preferably strawy stuff on heavy ground. But as many of us cannot obtain manure nowadays we are forced to use something else and this is where the compost heap comes into its own. Well-made compost is excellent even if it has not completely rotted down. Spread it around, two or three inches deep, such things as border plants, fruit trees, etc. Place it as shown in the insets, B being the right way and A the wrong way. The point about this is that it may well engender a certain amount of heat which would be harmful to the trunk of the tree.

It also has the advantage that it will rot down during the summer and can be dug in during the autumn to provide additional nourishment as well as improving the texture of the soil.

If you have no compost, you can perhaps gather leaf-mould or get some peat or even use grass-cuttings (but not if you have used weed-killer on the lawn). In fact, any plant material will do that contains no harmful chemicals.

In most cases a top-dressing of a general fertiliser, such as National Growmore, would benefit the plants. This should be sprinkled around before the mulch is put on. As the mulch keeps the ground moist the fertiliser will work its way down into the soil.

Mulching also saves work because you will need to do much less watering later on.

A similar programme can wisely be used with pot plants. Remove the top inch of soil and top dress with new compost, such as John Innes.

SWEET-PEAS

Provided the soil is in a suitable workable condition, we can now put out the sweet-pea plants raised under glass and hardened off.

For the best results you need a site which has been well-prepared, old manure or compost having been dug into the second spit and the top spit dressed with a general fertiliser such as Growmore. If you haven't already prepared such a site, do it now and defer planting out for a week or so. It is better to do such groundwork late than not to do it at all.

The young plants are placed 9 in. apart if to be grown in a row or about 6 in. apart if in a ring as shown in inset B. The tops should be pinched out, as in inset A, unless they have previously been stopped, to induce them to send up new, strong basal shoots. Always use a trowel for planting, never a dibber for plants such as these.

Placing the plants in a ring, as in B, is a good plan from the point of view of having decorative high-spots in the flower borders, especially when supported by twiggy sticks in the form of a cone.

For those who wish to grow them in a more professional way, rows are best, each plant having its own cane as a support, as in inset C, in order to achieve the best possible flowers for cutting or for showing. But this method is a lot more trouble as each plant is restricted to a single stem which is tied to its support regularly as it grows, the tendrils and side-shoots all being removed, to concentrate the plant's energy into flower production. Remove any flower buds that form before the plants are about 3 ft. high or until the flower-buds number at least four per stem.

While the plants are still young they seem to be a tasty salad for sparrows, so some form of protection such as netting or black cotton is advisable at this stage.

For those who have not been able to raise their own plants, seeds can be sown in the open ground if it is dry enough to crumble. Soak the seeds in water for 24 hours before sowing to make them swell and break the outer skin. The toughest skins are the black ones and if the soaking does not succeed in splitting them, scrape off a little on the side of the seed opposite the "eye", taking care not to damage the seed itself.

SWEET CORN

Have you tried growing Sweet Corn yet? Many more people are now doing so, particularly the younger folk, as it is one of those vegetables that is "in" among that section of the population.

For those with warm greenhouse or garden frame, seed can be sown now. Sow thinly in a box of seed-sowing compost or individually in 3 in. peat pots. If you sow in a box, the seedlings will need pricking out when large enough into 3 in. pots and if raised in a greenhouse will need transferring to a cold-frame for hardening off before planting out in permanent quarters in late May or early June. Sowing in peat pots avoids the process of pricking out.

The plants should be set out about a foot apart in several short rows, at least four, so as to form a square, the rows being 2 ft. apart. This arrangement is much better than planting in one long row, as is usual for most crops, as it improves the ratio of pollination.

If you wish to sow the seed out-of-doors, do not do so until mid-May. Sow in short rows to form a square, as before, and in due course thin out the seedlings until they are a foot apart in the row.

Once the plants are growing well, and they need rich, deeply dug soil (the sort of conditions you would provide for dahlias), make sure they have plenty of moisture, watering freely if necessary and adding liquid manure to the water twice a week, unless you know your ground has been richly dressed beforehand. Hoe regularly between the plants so that the surface never remains caked for long after the watering.

Nearly all the varieties offered for sale nowadays are F1 hybrids, which are a great improvement on the older varieties. Of these, probably the best is one called Early Extra Sweet. This can be eaten raw, cooked or stored in a freezer. It has the sweetness of a freshly-gathered young garden pea and is as easy to grow as the ordinary lettuce.

SOME UNUSUAL VEGETABLES

This year try some vegetables that you may not have grown before if you have the space in the garden. It will add variety to your menu, will provide crops when others may not be ready and introduce you to flavours you may not have tasted before.

Any good garden soil will do, provided it is broken down into a fine tilth suitable for seed sowing. Rake into the top few inches a dressing of Growmore fertiliser two weeks before drawing the drills.

Inset A shows one vegetable few people know or grow—Kohl-rabi. As this one is a member of the cabbage family, a dressing of lime would be advisable to ward off club-root disease. Sow this month or next thinly in shallow drills 15 in. apart. Thin out later to 9 in. apart. You eat the root when it has reached the size of a tennis-ball. Cook it in its "jacket" —don't peel it, to obtain the maximum of its nutty flavour.

Our second inset shows Globe Artichoke, in which it is the partially-opened flower-heads that are eaten. To grow these from seed, sow this month or next. When the seedlings are large enough to handle, transplant them about 12 in. apart and transfer them to their maturing positions the following spring, 3 ft. apart. They grow about 5 ft. high, are quite ornamental and can, therefore, be placed at the back of a plot, or even at the back of a flower border. They can then remain, undisturbed, for 3 years, yielding a crop each year.

Our third inset shows the curiously shaped Sweet Peppers which can be used in salads or for flavouring hot dishes. These need some protection. The seeds can be sown now in pots but these must be kept in a greenhouse or in the home. The plants can go outside in May or June but should have cloches placed over them. They must be kept growing continuously in warm conditions in nicely moist soil so that they mature as quickly as possible. The fruits all start out green but turn yellow and red as they ripen. They are best used when half-ripe. If you are not familiar with their flavour, use rather sparingly at first and increase, if you think fit, subsequently, so that your family and friends realise that you are giving your dishes a touch of Common Market culinary.

WINTER CAULIFLOWER

Quite a number of people have difficulty in growing cauliflowers successfully. This is no reflection on their methods of cultivation. The cauliflower is a difficult subject in many areas. It needs very rich soil, is not hardy and will never do well on dry soil or in hot summers. Moreover, when it does succeed, all the heads seem to mature at the same time. In these areas, or for the non-expert, the best advice is to stop trying the impossible and to switch to cauliflower-type Broccoli. This is not nearly so fussy about soil and conditions, is much more hardy and will give you mature heads for a large part of the year if you choose suitable varieties.

These varieties can be divided more or less into three groups—those that will mature in the autumn, those maturing next winter and those ready for use the following spring.

For use next autumn you could grow Veitch's Self-Protecting (a variety not needing leaves bent over the curd to protect it from frost). Christmas, as its name implies, comes next and Snow's Winter White is ready in Jan. and Feb. For Mar. and Apr. use St. George (shown in inset B), Early March or Purity. Matchless and Late Queen should cover the period from Apr. to June.

So we have covered most of the year except summer, when in any case there should be plenty of other vegetables to use.

All these varieties can be sown now. A good seed bed should be prepared and lime added unless your land is known to be sufficiently limy. Draw a drill about an inch deep, sow thinly and cover with fine soil. Thin them out early, as soon as they are large enough to handle, to prevent overcrowding, to ensure getting stocky, robust plants. When they are large enough, prick them out in boxes of good compost or in good soil in the garden and dust with an insecticide to ward off flea beetle.

By June or July you should have a good supply of fine plants to set out 2 ft. apart each way where they are to mature. Firm land, manured for a previous crop, suits them best. Use Calomel dust, as per maker's instructions, as protection against club root and cabbage root fly.

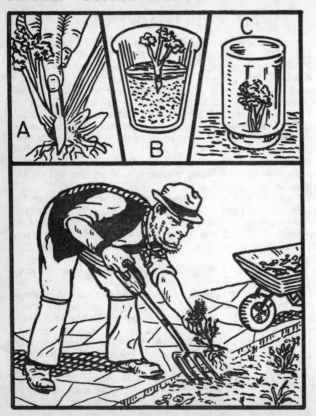

BORDER RENOVATION

The perennials in your herbaceous borders are now probably making good progress producing strong shoots, many of which can be used as cuttings if you want to increase your stock.

The borders should be lightly turned over, digging in any manure spread around the plants last autumn and at the same time removing the weeds. A border not manured in the autumn would benefit by the application now of a dressing of bone-meal or Growmore fertiliser. If your ground needs it, a dressing of lime could also be given. The improvement these dressings make will very soon be apparent.

As far as cuttings are concerned, we take the ever-popular delphinium as an example. It should be noted that the removal of a reasonable number of cuttings (2 out of 6, perhaps) from each plant will not be to that plant's detriment. On the contrary, it will probably improve the subsequent display as most of these plants produce more shoots than they can bring to really successful maturity.

To take the cuttings, scrape the soil away from the collar of the plant, preferably with the fingers so as not to harm the shoots. Cut off each shoot carefully, as low down as possible. If you can get it off with a few roots attached so much the better. Insert each shoot into a mixture of equal parts peat and sand in a half-filled pot of a suitable size. The heel of the cutting should be about an inch in the mixture.

Place the pots in a cold-frame and place the light in position. If you do not have a cold-frame, you can achieve similar conditions for your cuttings by inserting them in the same mixture in a box about 4 in. deep. Cover the top of the box with a sheet of glass. Water when necessary, regularly.

Within 3 or 4 weeks, these cuttings should have made a good root system in this mixture. As soon as they have, they must be planted out. Good as this mixture is for root formation, it does not contain any nourishment and the new plants will soon begin to suffer from starvation if left in it too long.

ZINNIAS

Zinnias provide us with such a wonderfully showy display of colour from mid-summer onwards that they are a justifiably popular half-hardy annual. But few people seem to grow them from seed. Most buy plants ready for bedding out in June. Of course, you cannot raise your own plants from seed ready for bedding out unless you have a heated greenhouse. A temperature of 55°F. (13°C.) is necessary and now is the time to sow the seed. It should be sown $\frac{1}{16}$ in. deep, the sort of impossible instruction I detest! Translate this into sowing on top of a good, moist seed compost and just cover the seed with a sprinkling of silver sand. Sow very thinly so that you can leave most of the plants in the box until they are large enough to pot up singly. This is to avoid pricking out into other boxes before potting up as Zinnias don't really like being disturbed. If you pot the seedlings singly they can be grown on until early May when the pots can be transferred to a cold frame. They should then be gradually hardened off until bedding out in June, about 8-12 in. apart.

Because of their dislike of being moved, good results can be obtained by sowing Zinnias where they are to grow. You want nice rich loam, previously enriched with decayed manure, in a really sunny spot. In May or June, when the soil has become thoroughly warm, sow as before. Thin out later as necessary and feed with liquid manure when the buds show.

There are lots of attractive varieties. For example, inset A shows the so-called dahlia-flowered type, large double blooms ranging in colour from white and yellow to orange, scarlet and purple. Inset B shows one called Sombrero, single blooms $2\frac{1}{2}$ in. across of scarlet, yellow-tipped petals.

There is another variety, an F1 hybrid, called Peter Pan, in two shades—"warm coral pink" and "glowing rosy-carmine". This produces its first bloom (4 in. across!) when the plant is only about 6 in. high. This bloom is followed by others, more or less continuously, from basal branches, for the rest of the summer. But these blooms are rather smaller.

FRENCH BEANS

By comparison with runners, French beans are, I think, undeservedly neglected by some people. On a given area of land the crop from French beans is greater than you get from runners. You may say you prefer the flavour of runners (my wife does) but I maintain that French beans have a distinct flavour of their own which is decidedly pleasant, despite being different from that of runners.

Out-of-doors we can make a start with a sowing at the end of this month in the South. In the North, it would be wiser to wait until the middle of May. Draw a drill 1½ in. deep and in it sow the seeds 9 in. apart, leaving 18 in. between rows if sowing more than one. I don't sow more than one row at a time, believing it to be better to sow at fortnightly intervals, so that they do not all mature at once. Of course, if you have a deep freeze and can pop the surplus crop into that, successional sowing doesn't matter. But for freezing you must grow a suitable variety as not all of them will freeze satisfactorily. Remus is a good variety for this purpose, having the added advantage that it bears its pods *above* the foliage.

Of course, if you want to produce some really early crops, and can spare the space, you can sow some in a cold-frame or in pots in the greenhouse. Half-a-dozen seeds in an 8 in. pot grown in a temperature of 60°F. (15-16°C.) using potting compost such as John Innes No. 3 will provide a surprisingly large number of pods.

Have you ever tried eating French beans raw in a salad? Picked fresh from the garden when a good size but still young, washed and sliced, they add a flavour to a salad which people seldom fail to comment on as it is unlike that of any other vegetable and is usually assumed to be something exotic and Continental. Here again, Remus is an outstanding variety for salad use.

STRAWBERRIES

According to my wife, there is one garden product of which a family never has a surplus—and that is the strawberry. So let us do our best to meet the demand as they will be quite pricey, I am sure, when they are offered for sale—even on the basis of "pick-your-own".

By now the plants should be growing quite strongly. Give them a dressing of National Growmore fertiliser or one of these formulated manures that are so popular nowadays. Apply according to directions on the container and then hoe it into the surface soil. Don't hoe very deeply or very closely to the plants as all their roots are in the top six inches of soil.

There are, commonly, two principal disease or pest problems with strawberries. One is powdery mildew on the leaves, particularly the undersides. For this dust the plants thoroughly with a powder puffer of flowers of sulphur. Do this even before any mildew is seen as it does have a preventive effect but certainly repeat the application immediately you do see any signs of mildew.

The other problem is a pest called the seed beetle. For this, sink a jam-jar or two among the plants and drop a small piece of meat, about the size of a half-inch cube, into each jar. The beetles, seeking the meat, fall in and cannot get out again. You can then easily destroy them as soon as they are seen. These beetles feed only at night.

The next step in our production programme is to surround the plants with straw or some suitable substitute, such as the special mats sold for this purpose, black polythene, peat, or even grass cuttings, if you have nothing better. But *don't* use cuttings from a lawn which has been treated with a weed-killer. Having thus taken steps to ensure that the fruit is kept clean, you must now outwit those determined poachers, the blackbirds and others, who are also very partial to strawberries. So cover all the plants with nets, supported well above the fruit, so that the wife will always be able to pick a sufficiency of fine fruit when the time comes.

HALF-HARDY ANNUALS

Even if you only have a greenhouse or garden frame without heat you can still raise your own half-hardy annuals..

Use a John Innes compost or one of the soil-less ones. Or, if you want to mix your own, use two parts of good loam, one of leaf-mould, and one of sand. Mix thoroughly, fill your boxes, pans, pots, etc., and water well. When these containers have drained well, say overnight in the house or frame, sprinkle the seed on top. Just cover with fine soil or sand.

Never let the mixture dry out. On the other hand, don't make it too wet because there is always the danger of the seedlings "damping-off" in the rather humid atmosphere they favour. If you see the slightest sign of this, use Cheshunt Compound according to directions. Or, better still, use it anyway, as prevention is better than cure and it usually seems to give the seedlings added vigour.

These seedlings will later on (when they have their first pair of true leaves) need pricking out separately into other boxes of good compost if you have a garden big enough to take a large number of plants. If you haven't you can just thin them out, leaving, of course, the most sturdy specimens and discarding the others.

Boxes of pricked-out seedlings need at least a couple of weeks standing out in the open to harden off before being planted out at the end of May or early June.

Many of these half-hardy annuals can be grown from outdoor sowings, like the hardy annuals, if not sown before late May or early June. In fact, it is quite a good plan to grow some each way so as to prolong the flowering display. Those that can be sown direct into their flowering positions are usually so marked in seed catalogues.

The insets show: A is an Aster, Pepito Mixed—semi-double marguerite-type blooms in vivid colours. B is Bartonia Aurea, one of the most brilliant annuals, golden yellow, which is one that can be sown direct in the open ground, as it is fully hardy in many parts of the country. C is an even earlier-flowering variety of the ever-popular scarlet Salvia, called Tom Thumb.

GREENHOUSE TOMATOES

Tomato plants raised from seed in a heated greenhouse will now be reaching the stage when they are to go into their permanent fruiting positions. (This does not apply to those people who grow their tomatoes out-of-doors. Their plants are not put out until June.)

In the greenhouse, the plants can go straight into the greenhouse border if you wish, but there is a lot to be said for growing them by the ring culture method. This merely means placing each plant in a special container, usually a strip of paper treated with bitumen stapled together to form a short cylinder without a bottom.

The plant is set in a potting compost such as John Innes No. 3, or one of the soil-less composts. The rings are then stood on a bed, at least 6 in. deep, of well-weathered ash, or some equally porous material, such as vermiculite or small gravel.

If this porous bed is made in a trench, when you have placed the rings in position the spaces between them can be filled with some of the soil taken out when digging the trench.

If the bed is made up on the greenhouse floor, with a board in front to keep it in position, fill up spaces between rings with some light material.

This same ash-based trench and ring culture method can be used for outdoor plants with advantage—in June.

When the plants are first set in position be careful not to overdo the watering. Provide each plant with a suitably strong support and keep all side-shoots pinched out as shown in inset but, of course, be careful not to remove the tiny flowering stems.

Once the first truss of fruit has set, start feeding. Use according to the maker's instructions which usually means a moderate feed every 10-14 days, watered into the rings. The ash base must also be kept moist.

In this way the plants develop two root systems. One, mainly fibrous, in the rings, taking up the nourishment provided, and another, more tap-root like, taking up moisture from the ash base.

The most important rule is that the compost and roots in the rings must be kept nicely moist at all times.

51

BRUSSELS SPROUTS

Brussels sprouts sown under glass earlier in the year must be properly hardened off in a cold-frame before being planted out in the open ground next month.

Club root is a disease that must be guarded against with this crop. If you know from past experience that you are free of this problem, keep the ball of soil around each plant's roots intact when planting out. If not, shake off the soil and dip the roots in soil, soot and water mixed to the consistency of double cream before putting the plants in position. An even better safeguard is a paste of 4 per cent calomel dust and water.

In any case, unless your ground is known to be well supplied with lime, sprinkle a little into each hole and mix it with the soil before planting.

To ensure getting nice stocky plants that have developed good root systems, put the plants out about 4 in. apart first of all. Then, when they are about 6 in. high transplant them at least 2 ft. apart in their permanent positions.

Brussels need soil in good heart, preferably manured last autumn, that is really firm, not freshly dug. Whether manured or not, rake into the surface, before planting, a dressing, 2 oz. per square yard, of a general fertiliser, such as Growmore.

Make the holes, with a trowel, deep enough to allow the roots to assume their normal position when the plants are lowered in, right up to their first leaves. Make them really firm with the fingers or the trowel handle. If necessary, water them and keep nicely moist until they are obviously well-established. After that, you need only keep them weeded, loosening only the top inch of soil with the hoe regularly, and provide stakes to keep them upright if needed. Inset B shows how they should crop—very close together on the stem.

If you haven't yet made a start with Brussels it is not too late. You won't get an early crop, but a late one is better than none at all, if you sow seed now.

LEEKS

Like Brussels, dealt with earlier, leeks are a very valuable crop for use in winter (November to March) when vegetables are scarce—and expensive. They are particularly useful in cold areas as they withstand severe conditions extremely well. In these circumstances, lifting them can be a problem because they have to be left in the ground until required as they will not store. Nevertheless, they should be more widely grown, outside those areas where their cultivation is almost a religion.

Seed can be sown now in a bed raked very fine. Sow thinly and shallowly as one would onions. Transplant when they are large enough, any time from June to August.

When you lift the plants, cut back the foliage slightly, as shown in inset A. Any long, straggling roots can also be shortened to the general length of the others.

Good, rich soil is needed and in this take out a trench 5 or 6 in. deep. In the trench make dibber holes 6 in. deep, 9 in. apart and drop a plant in each. The plants are then watered in; they aren't really planted, the water washing soil around them being sufficient. Rows should be 18 in. apart. About three-quarters of the plant is covered in this way.

Later, as they grow, soil from the sides of the trench is pulled up to the plants with a hoe or rake to keep the light from the stems to blanch them. This can be done in stages as they develop height. This method is a lot less trouble than tying special collars of cardboard, etc., round each one to achieve the same result. But I must say that one man I know found a very easy blanching method—he just stood a land drain pipe over each plant! And it worked!

If you can spread peat about an inch deep round each plant it will prevent weeds growing and the leeks will appreciate it. Thoroughly water them once a week—particularly in dry weather—with liquid manure.

Another good tip is to apply sulphate of ammonia—2 oz. per yard run—before you do the first earthing up—it gives them a tremendous boost.

HONEYSUCKLE—THE SWEET SCENT OF SUMMER

THERE is surely nothing more pleasant in the garden in June than to sense the perfume of the honeysuckle carried on the warm evening air.

But its fragrance is not something which can only be enjoyed on early summer evenings. There are honeysuckles which flower in winter and others which bloom in early autumn.

There are honeysuckles from China and honeysuckles from Canada. In all there are around 200 different kinds. Some are not even climbers at all, but shrubs.

Honeysuckles are for every garden. For, whether your walls, or fences face north, south, east or west, there is a suitable honeysuckle. Ideally they like their roots in the shade and their heads in the sun, and they grow both up and along a wall or fence.

Some honeysuckles, despite their family name, are scentless. But they often more than make up for this loss in really beautiful flowers.

For instance, most people's idea of a honeysuckle is a green-leafed climber with whorls of pale yellow flowers suffused with purple.

Our native honeysuckle, or woodbine, is just such a plant. And it gives great pleasure whether you see it on a house wall or rambling through a country hedgerow.

Yet did you know that you can have honeysuckles with scarlet, purple, pink and orange flowers?

The Trumpet Honeysuckle is a beautiful, partly deciduous plant—it may lose all its leaves in winter if the weather is nasty—which originated in the United States. Given a favourable position in the south and west of Britain, it can reach an impressive 20ft. in height.

It produces clusters of three-inch long trumpet shaped flowers from June to August. The "trumpets" are orange-scarlet outside and mustard yellow inside. And their scent is gorgeous.

In eastern areas, where the Trumpet Honeysuckle would not succeed because of the winter cold, you can grow the scented hybrid Brown's Honeysuckle. It has similar shaped scarlet flowers from June to August and is quite hardy. But instead of growing to 20ft., this one is more likely to settle for a more modest 10ft., which could well prove to be an additional advantage.

Both of these honeysuckles are best grown on south facing walls.

Yet another honeysuckle for a south wall or fence is the Mediterranean honeysuckle called Etrusca, which will attain 10-15ft. in height. It has very fragrant yellow flowers tinged with red which go on blooming from July to October.

However, if you do have simpler tastes, then I suggest that you grow one of the two varieties of our native honeysuckle. In fact some folk might well argue that it is the best.

Belgica is the early flowering red and yellow form which comes into bloom in May and continues right through June into July. Then there is Serotina. Its flowers are purple and cream and they put in an appearance in July and are still there to please you in September.

Both of these honeysuckles are deliciously scented and should be given a north, east or west aspect. They grow at least 10ft. tall.

Some nurserymen advertise Belgica and Serotina as Early Dutch and Late Dutch Honeysuckles which is worth knowing if you cannot find them listed under the names I have given. Why Dutch? Well you know what keen gardeners they are in Holland.

For smaller gardens, where a rampant climber might quickly prove an embarrassment, you are best to choose a less vigorous variety such as Goldflame, and grow it against a house wall. This reaches about 10ft., and has rosy purple, wax-like flowers from July to October. This particular honeysuckle produces show after show of new blooms for its entire four-month flowering period.

Dropmore Scarlet also grows to about 10ft. and its whorls of flowers from July to October are not unlike those of the exotic Trumpet Honeysuckle. This one, unfortunately, is pretty but scentless.

If limiting the growth of a honeysuckle is your problem —pruning often only makes matters worse—the alternative to a less vigorous variety is to plant the honeysuckle in an 8- or 10-inch *clay* pot.

This pot can then be filled with ordinary garden soil, the honeysuckle planted and the pot sunk up to its rim in the soil at the spot where you want the honeysuckle to grow.

The pot must be clay to enable moisture to travel in and out.

You can also stand a large pot or a tub close to a wall or fence and grow a honeysuckle in that if, for example, there is concrete right up to a house wall.

Of the honeysuckles which I have suggested, nearly all lose most of their leaves in winter. But if you want an evergreen kind to hide a shed, fence or ugly brick wall, then you have the choice of the purple flowered Henry's Honeysuckle, Halliana or the Japanese Honeysuckle.

However, no matter which one you choose, all honeysuckles like the same sort of growing conditions: good loamy soil which retains enough moisture to keep their roots cool. If your soil is not like that, then it should be enriched with some garden compost or peat.

Before planting, which can be done now, give a little thought to the growing supports for your honeysuckle, because, although the honeysuckle is described as a "climber", it is incapable of gripping a brick wall without a few "fingerholds".

In the past gardeners perhaps put up a framework of wires. But it is far better I think to use one of the plastic or plastic covered metal trellises. These give a honeysuckle all the support it needs and the trellises (white, brown or green) are more attractive than a motley assortment of wires.

I have never been one for forecasting the weather, but I can tell you this much: With the right honeysuckle, come rain or shine, you are in for a sweet and balmy summer . . .

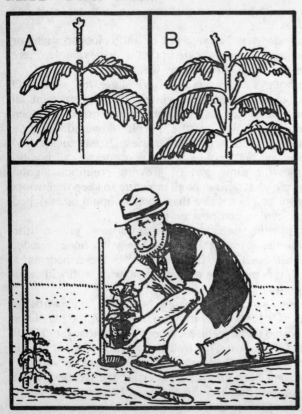

OUTDOOR CHRYSANTHEMUMS

Provided outdoor chrysanthemum plants have been properly hardened off—which means that they have been in a cold-frame for at least three weeks if you have raised your own plants from cuttings—they can now go out into their permanent positions in the garden unless the weather is unusually adverse.

The bed should have already had a good helping of manure or compost dug in well below the surface. Before putting in the plants, spread over the surface a half-inch dressing of moist peat, plus a sprinkling of a good general fertiliser such as National Growmore. Hoe these lightly into the surface, nicely levelling the bed.

Take out a hole of an adequate size for each plant with a trowel. Then drive in at the side of the hole a good firm cane 5 or 6 ft. in length, with at least a foot in the ground. Keep the ball of soil round the roots of each plant intact as it comes out of its pot and plant so that the top of the ball of soil is just below the surface of the surrounding soil. Plant firmly, pressing in with the fingers. Tie each plant to its support.

The plants should have been watered before being removed from their pots and if the bed is reasonably moist they will not need watering in.

After about 10 days, when it should be obvious that they are established, pinch out the growing tip, as shown in inset A. The plants should then be about six inches high. This pinching-out should result in at least three side shoots developing, as shown in inset B. These are the shoots that produce the blooms.

Many growers flower the plants on these three shoots, pinching out any others that develop in order to produce first-class blooms. You can grow on more than three shoots if you prefer to have more blooms of a smaller size, rather than just three full-size ones. Or you can, later on, pinch out the tips of the original three, and allow each to produce three further shoots so that you will have nine blooms per plant. This is quite a good plan as the blooms will be a good size but they will, of course, be later in flowering.

FRUIT SPRAYING

In our grow-your-own-food programme this year, we should take positive steps to ensure that pests and diseases do not spoil the fruit of our labours.

One of those steps is the timely spraying of fruit trees. The timing is determined by the stage reached by the trees, not by the calendar. These stages are shown in the insets, the first being what we call the green cluster stage, the next the pink bud (white bud in pears), the third petal fall and the last the fruitlet stage.

The best plan is to spray at all four stages, as they are reached. However, if you gave your trees a winter wash, as recommended in December, you can omit spraying at the green cluster stage. If you *are* spraying at this stage use Orthocide or lime-sulphur. Either of these can be used at the next stage, white bud on pears and pink on apples, and for the fourth stage, when the fruitlets have formed. But for the third stage, petal fall, use a systemic insecticide. In this way we do our best to combat both diseases and pests.

Don't spray during a cold spell or when the weather is windy or wet. I should also give a word of warning about lime-sulphur. Some varieties of apples, for example Newton Wonder and Beauty of Bath as well as some pears, such as Doyenne du Comice, are sulphur shy. So if you are in any doubt about the varieties you have, use Orthocide, not lime-sulphur.

The insecticide you use at the third stage can wisely be repeated later on as per instructions on container, in May, June and July, particularly if any evidence of aphides or other pests is seen.

Finally, remember that similar protection should be given to currants, raspberries, strawberries, etc., always carefully following the maker's instructions. In all cases it is particularly important to spray the *under*sides of leaves, as that is usually where the enemy lurks.

ONE MAN WENT TO MOW . . .

The lawn-mowing season is now in full swing, with lawns where the grass is growing rapidly being cut twice a week. This may sound like a lot of work but is, in fact, a labour-saving method. A lawn that is cut every three or four days (during May and June, usually, when the rate of grass-growth justifies it) can be cut *with ease,* plus a certain amount of pleasure and pride.

Hacking away at an over-grown lawn is not only very hard work, it is also very bad for the lawn.

Using a side-wheel or roller hand mower with a push and pull motion because you cannot go straight ahead is a sure indication that the grass is too long or you are trying to cut it too short. Electric or motor-driven mowers may cope with this situation but you are still doing harm to the lawn.

The remedy if the grass has been allowed to get too long is to cut it twice. Raise the cut by adjusting the mower so that you take off first of all just the top of the grass. leave it for a day so that the grass stands up again, adjust the mower for a lower cut and do it again. From then on, cut regularly, before it gets out of hand again. And don't cut the grass too short. For the average home lawn, the grass should never be cut shorter than one inch, even in the summer. In spring, autumn or during a very dry spell in summer $1\frac{1}{4}$ in. is short enough, from the point of view of a healthy lawn. Even for a tip-top quality lawn half an inch in summer is the minimum grass length and $\frac{3}{4}$ in. at other seasons.

Another lawn fallacy concerns the use of a roller. You *cannot* level a lawn by rolling it. A roller makes little impression on the high spots and tends to accentuate the depressions. This is because the high spots are drier and harder than the low places which remain wet and soft.

An easy way of levelling is shown in the insets. Insert a spade at an angle of 45° on each side of a strip as shown. Then raise the piece in a curve by the use of two forks. Then add or remove soil under the turf to correct the level. Press turf into position again and the repair will soon be invisible.

TOMATO TIPS

Most gardeners are keen to get their out-door tomato plants into their fruiting positions as soon as possible. But this is a case where more haste can mean less speed as the tomato plant is extremely sensitive to temperature change. At the present time, the plants should be hardening off ready for planting out at the end of this month or early next, according to the weather.

If you are going to buy plants, try to find out whether they have been properly hardened-off—and choose plants that are short and sturdy and have dark green leaves—paleness indicates that they have come from glass-protected conditions or have been raised too fast in too much heat.

One job that can be done now is the preparation of the site where the plants are to go—preferably in a row on the sunny side of a wall or fence where they will get protection from wind and the reflected warmth of the sun. Assuming the soil is nicely fertile, having been previously enriched with manure or fertiliser, dig it over mixing in a good dressing of bonfire ash.

When you put out the plants, set them 1½ ft. apart and just sufficiently deep that the top roots are no more than ½ in. below the surface. Dig each hole with a trowel and place each plant in it carefully, keeping the ball of soil intact. Make each plant nicely firm with the fingers. Drive in a good strong cane at the same time so that you are sure it is not harming the roots. Each plant should be tied, not too tightly, to its support. If the ground is dry, water each one after planting and then give no more water for a week. Proper watering is a very important process for successful tomato growing. It must be adequate to ensure even moisture content in the soil and must be done regularly. A good mulch around the plants of manure or compost is very advantageous.

All side-shoots must be picked out regularly as soon as they get about an inch in length; making sure you do not pick out the tiny bunches of flower-buds, of course.

Feeding the plants with a special fertiliser pays good dividends. Do not start until the fruit on the first truss has set.

59

PLANT RE-POTTING

The question of when to re-pot a house plant is one which bothers a lot of readers. The best way to ascertain the root situation of any pot plant is to turn the pot upside-down and to tap the edge on a bench so as to remove the pot. You can then easily examine the roots. If a mass of tiny roots is found to be going round and round the ball of soil, then the plant needs re-potting as a general rule. And in many cases it is as well to do it now, unless it happens to be a plant that is in full bloom. In that case, leave the re-potting until after it has finished blooming.

Next comes the question of pot size. Never use a pot too large. Move on to the next size. In other words, move from a 5 in. pot to a 6 in., or a 6 in. to a 7 in. The reason for this is shown in the insets. B shows a plant from a 3 in. pot moved into a 5 in. one (4 in. pots are seldom used nowadays). The plant then has a reasonable amount of new soil in which to develop naturally, pushing its tiny rootlets out into the new compost. If a plant is moved into too large a pot the main roots take full advantage of the abundance of new nourishment and grow straight out to the sides of the pot as shown in inset A. The rootlets then start searching for food round and round the soil ball and you have a repetition of the situation you had in the original pot.

Use one of the excellent soil-less potting composts or John Innes No. 2. It should be moist but not really wet.

After re-potting, water only moderately and stand the plants in a moister and shadier position than normal for the first week or ten days. Once they have obviously recovered from the move they can be fully watered and replaced in their original positions.

Another important factor in the process is hygiene. Just as when making up your own compost, you should use sterilised soil, you should also ensure that all the pots you are going to use are sterile. Scrub all of them—particularly clay ones—in a bucket of disinfectant diluted in water—instructions about quantity should be on the container—putting the pots in the bucket to soak for a while before you scrub each one clean.

MARROWS

If you already have marrow seedlings ready to put out, wait until all danger of frost has passed, unless you can protect them with cloches until about the end of June.

If you do not have any plants, there is still time to sow seed, preferably in a warm greenhouse or room, three seeds to a pot. Alternatively, sow a couple of seeds in a warm spot out-of-doors and cover with a sheet of glass or a jam-jar.

For the pot, use a soil-less or John Innes seed compost. Unless you have unusually good soil, use a potful of the same compost in a hole for sowing out-of-doors.

Each bush marrow—the type I recommend you to grow—needs about one square yard of ground, or, as is usually done, a circle one yard in diameter. This should be dug out two spits deep, keeping the top spit separate. Mix about half the second spit with an equal quantity of manure. To eke out your precious manure you can substitute for some of it, rotted leaves or lawn mowings (NOT from a weed-killer treated lawn!). Add a sprinkling of bone-meal to this mixture and return it to the hole. Now return the top soil, arranging the surface in the shape of a saucer, in the centre of which the marrow plant will be placed when there is no longer any frost danger.

This plant must be kept well watered at all times but never saturated so that the soil becomes waterlogged.

As soon as the young marrows form, substitute liquid manure for the water.

If you find the female flowers are falling off without setting, the bees, etc., are not doing their stuff. You must then pollinate the female flowers yourself, picking male flowers to brush pollen on to the female ones. (You can recognise the female flowers by the slightly "pregnant" stem behind the flower-head.) And do your fatherhood act before noon—flowers and pollen are then still bedewed and more likely to stay together.

And do eat your babies while they are still young. If your thumb-nail will not easily penetrate the skin they're too old.

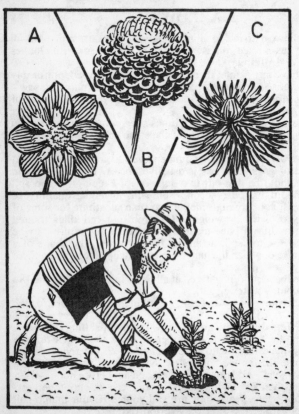

DAHLIAS

For an outstanding display of bloom, few flowers equal the dahlia.

Those who have raised plants in pots from cuttings and those who are buying new plants can now set them in their flowering positions, providing the weather is normal for the time of year. If it is not, wait a week or two as dahlias are very susceptible to low night temperatures.

The bed where they are to be planted should have been well-manured in the autumn or early spring. But in any case scatter a good handful per square yard of a general fertiliser such as Growmore over the surface before planting. Do this now, whether you are planting immediately or not.

Water the pots well before removing the plants. Knock each one out carefully, keeping the ball of soil round the roots intact if you can. Make a sufficiently large hole with a trowel so that the top of this soil ball is about 2 in. below the surface. Provide each plant with a good strong stake at the same time. Plant firmly and water well in.

After planting, a mulch two or three inches deep around each plant, but not letting it rest against the stem, is a great advantage. The soil to be covered should be wet before the mulch is put down. Few of us can get horse manure nowadays, but if you can get, as some people can, cow or pig manure (or a mixture of both) use this as it is very suitable for dahlias. But it should be well rotted, having stood in a heap for at least a year.

When the plants are well established in their new positions and have at least three *pairs* of leaves, nip out the growing point. This makes them develop side-shoots and produce bushy plants. To this end, it may be necessary to pinch out any early-developing flower buds, but eventual flower production will be much greater for this sacrifice.

There is a vast variety to choose from. The insets show just three. "A" is a collarette "Libretto", red outer petals, white inner ones, plus a golden centre: "B" shows a miniature ball, up to 4 in. across, red, called "Rothesay Superb", and "C" shows "Drakenburg", purple-bronze, a large-flowered cactus type 8 to 10 in. across.

HOLIDAY PREPARATIONS

A few simple precautions taken before you go on holiday will save much backache (and heartache) when you return.

One of the principal problems is the lawn, if you cannot arrange for someone to cut it for you while you are away. Cut it, if possible, the day before you leave and cut it as short as you dare without harming it. If your soil is the sort which you fear will become too dry while you are away, take off the grass-box and leave the cuttings on the surface as a protection against the sun.

If you do remove the cuttings, or if you have a supply on the compost heap already, use these to mulch certain crops like runner beans, tomatoes, etc., for which moist surface soil is essential. But the ground should be wet, heavily watering it if necessary, before the mulch is put on. If the grass cuttings are not wet, watering these after application will be helpful. Keep the cuttings away from direct contact with the plant stems.

Another important point, for those who grow their own vegetables, is to pick all crops, such as peas or beans, that are mature or will mature during your absence. Even if you cannot use them all yourself you can give them to friends and neighbours. This is much better than letting them spoil and thus retard the development of further supplies for your own use on your return. Salad crops, lettuces, etc., should be similarly treated.

The same principle applies in the flower garden. Cut off all blooms that are fully open or nearly so, to prevent the plants wasting their substance on seed-production, which in turn may well prevent or delay the formation of further flowers. Think how your neighbours will appreciate a nice bouquet.

House plants must, of course, be prevented from drying out. Place them in water as shown in inset. Others that you may not need back in the house when you return may be plunged up to their rims in a shady part of the garden itself. Having soil round the pots keeps them cool and moist and the plants will benefit from their holiday.

WATER GARDENING

DOES YOUR garden have that certain sparkle, the joy and the beauty which only water can bring?

Can you look out this morning at a pool where the surface is suddenly broken by a flash of blue and silver as a Japanese Nishiki Koi carp rises to take a fly?

Are the leaves of the exotic water lilies beginning to unfold on the water's surface? Are the golden marsh marigolds still blooming profusely among the luxuriant green leaves with their purplish sheen?

Is the fountain gently cascading water like thousands of molten silver droplets on to the shimmering surface of the pool?

A pool with plants and fish certainly does wonders for a garden. You can forget your prize roses, dahlias and sweet peas. If you have a pool, I know for sure what the main point of interest in your garden will be.

Some of the loveliest plants in the world are aquatic plants. I don't think there is any flower to beat the exquisite beauty of the water lily; and without a pool you will never have the chance to grow it.

Constructing a pool nowadays is simplicity itself, due to the development of plastic sheeting for the necessary watertight lining. Concrete, with its usually attendant leaks, is now seldom used.

And these new plastic "liners", as they are called, have a life expectancy of 50 years. In fact, with some liners, you get a 15-year guarantee.

The flexibility of the liners enables you to decide what *shape* of pool *you* want. It can be round, oval, rectangular, square or kidney-shaped. And great depth is unnecessary: 2ft. is enough for most water lilies (there are plenty which are quite happy in 15in.), with raised areas in the pool, where the water is only 6in. deep to suit marginal aquatic plants. The latter are the sort of plants you would find in the wild, growing at the edge of lakes, lochs and loughs.

A pool can be any *size* you want it to be. However, if you want to have a fair number of fish and different plants, then around 40 square feet of pool surface area is what you should aim for.

Such a pool would cost you £21 for the liner, £8 for plants, £4 for plastic planting crates and hessian squares (to prevent soil seeping into the pool).

You would also have to reckon on spending at least £6 for a dozen fancy fish. The cost of a fountain depends on how elaborate an arrangement you want, but for £20 you should be able to obtain the sort of sparkling, murmuring spray which is so soothing on hot summer days.

With such a pool it is unnecessary to rush out and spend £60 right away. You could start with the pool and plants and add the fish and fountain later.

A pool should be sited where it will be away from overhanging trees, as fallen leaves pollute the water, and where it will get at least half a day's sunshine.

You should buy the liner, plants and fish from one of the specialist water garden firms, who will also supply you with very simple, illustrated instructions on how to construct the pool.

The real work involved is in digging out the hole, which is why I suggest that you do not make the pool too deep. But even taking it easy, there is no reason why you should not manage the entire job in a couple of weekends.

Once the liner has been put in, the pool should be edged with some paving slabs or even bricks set flush with the level of your lawn.

The best time to instal aquatic plants in a pool is from now to September, and your pool—in addition to the water lilies and marginal plants that I have already mentioned—should contain floating plants and oxygenating plants to keep the water fresh and clear.

In a pool with a proper balance of plants and fish there are generally few problems. It should never, for instance, be necessary to change the water. So doing will introduce mineral salts from the mains water supply which will encourage the formation of green algae. In summer, of course, the pool may need topping up once a week to counteract evaporation.

The best planting material for aquatic plants is ordinary garden soil, and the greater the clay content, the better. Fertilisers are generally positively harmful, except in the case of water lilies, where slow-release sachets of Lily Grow can be inserted in the planting crates to provide the necessary phosphates essential for maximum floral display.

Water lilies come in snowy white, and in many shades of pink, red, yellow and copper, and, except for some of the rarer species, are hardy enough to be grown anywhere in Britain.

My favourites are the red Escarboucle, the scented, star-shaped delicate shell-pink Odorata W. B. Shaw and the primrose yellow Marliacea Chromatella.

How appropriate then that the botanical name for a water lily should be Nymphea. Like a young and beautiful woman, the attraction of the water lily lies in its obvious freshness and its sheer simplicity: in this case the elegantly shaped petals.

The water lily may be the star of the pool, but the supporting cast of plants such as the water hyacinth, iris, lavender musk, water hawthorn and various reeds, all add up to one of the greatest gardening shows on earth.

Even the fish have a part to play. As well as being extremely decorative and fun for adults and children alike, they feed on larvae and aquatic insects which otherwise could prove to be pests.

If you are unable to collect those fish yourself, they can be sent to you in plastic containers.

In the very coldest parts of the country a small £4 pool heater (or a floating block of wood) will enable you to keep a small area free of ice in winter, thus allowing poisonous gases to escape and fresh oxygen to enter the water.

Is it any wonder then that with such a magnificent feature in the garden, some people choose to extend the show into the evening by spending £17 to instal floating pool lighting ir red, blue, green or amber.

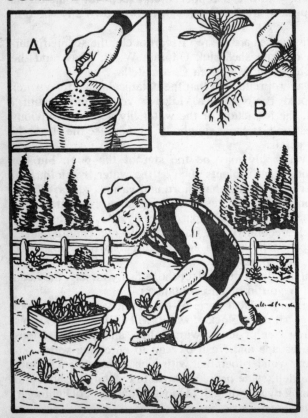

SALADS NON-STOP

One of the ways we can obtain the maximum benefit from a vegetable plot as a contribution to the household expenses is by producing salad plants non-stop throughout the season. As lettuce form a major part of nearly all salads concentrate on these.

The ideal soil for lettuces is fairly light, rich, deeply dug and well manured in a sunny position. I know only too well that in many gardens such a requirement is like asking for the moon. But do all you can to bring your selected lettuce area as near that ideal as you can and you will be handsomely repaid for your trouble.

Many people make the mistake of sowing far too much seed at one time. They then have masses of plants that mature all at once with the result that many of them "bolt", that is, run to seed before they can be used and end up on the compost heap.

If you sow in the open ground, sow only a short row, thin out early or lift some of the plants and plant them out elsewhere, 9 in. apart. The transplanted ones will probably mature a fortnight later than those left undisturbed.

A good tip is shown in inset B. Before planting, cut off about a third of the tap-root of each plant, provided there are plenty of fine roots above the cut. This has the effect of inducing earlier hearting. Which reminds me that it isn't really necessary to wait until the plants have produced really firm hearts before using them. Pull alternate plants as soon as they are large enough to use as in this way you'll save more money. By the time yours have hearted, they'll be lower in price in the shops anyway.

To save space in the garden, sow a pinch of seed in a large pot of good compost (see inset A), every two or three weeks, so that you always have fresh plants for planting out whenever you have available space. They can be put out as soon as the third normal leaf has formed and they can go in the spaces where you have already pulled plants for use, as suggested above, if you do not have other space available.

CELERY

As for lettuces, deeply dug, heavily manured soil is needed for celery—only more so! In fact, if you cannot provide such soil, grow something else on it!

A trench 15 to 18 in. wide, 15 in. deep should be taken out and 6 in. of good manure (a man-made substitute if you cannot get the natural product) dug into the bottom. Cover this with 6 in. of the best of the top soil.

Prepare the trench in this way as long before you are going to put in the plants as possible to let it weather and settle.

The spare soil is placed in a flat-topped mound on either side of the trench and on these mounds you can plant lettuces, as they will mature before you need to use the soil for earthing up the celery.

The plants can be set in the trench any time this month or next, 6 to 9 in. apart, in a single row in a 15 in.-wide trench, or in a double row in an 18-in. trench. Water in well after planting and keep them really moist by flooding the trench at intervals, particularly during a dry spell of weather.

When the plants are about 10 in. high, tie each one round the top to keep the leaf stalks together and so prevent earth falling into the heart. Then earth up as shown in inset A, noting the concave top to ensure that rain still gets down to the roots.

When the plants are nearly fully grown earth up again, as in inset B, with a convex top this time, so that the greatest possible length of stem is blanched by being kept in the dark by the earth. Nowadays most celery seed is treated to prevent what is called Celery Leaf Disease but it is still advisable to spray the plants with Bordeaux Mixture from August onwards.

Best results are obtained if you supplement their diet by applying a liquid fertiliser at 10-day intervals right through the growing season. Any side shoots produced should be removed right up to the period of first earthing-up.

HANGING BASKETS

I am sure no-one needs telling how attractive well-planted hanging baskets can be, but some guidance on their preparation and care may be welcome. The greatest problem is usually in keeping the soil sufficiently moist, as a basket hanging in mid-air obviously dries out more quickly than soil in a normal position. For this reason, the basic preparation is all-important. From an appearance point of view the outside is best packed tightly with moss. Inside this, place a piece of polythene, cut to size and shape, as this holds the moisture. Unfortunately, we must make a few drainage holes in the lower part of this polythene, otherwise we would have a stagnant muddy mess at the bottom of the basket in which the plants' roots would soon rot. (See insets A and B).

For the filling of the basket, John Innes compost No. 2 is very suitable, but I prefer to use a mixture of 3 parts of J.I. No. 2 and 1 part peat. This again is to have a compost that retains moisture better, as not all of us can give such baskets daily attention, which is what they really need, unless they hang in a position where they receive rain.

The best way of watering a basket is to take it down and stand it on a flower-pot in a bath of water so that the water soaks up from the bottom and sides. This ensures that the compost gets wet right through, in contrast to watering it overhead when much of the water merely runs out over the sides without wetting the ball of soil in the centre.

The planting of a basket is largely a matter of personal preference, of course, but it is usually wise to have one principal, upright centre plant, such as a fuchsia or large geranium (zonal pelargonium) surrounded by trailing plants, such as ivy-leafed geraniums or trailing lobelia. Modern petunias are one of my favourites for hanging baskets.

If watering baskets hanging high up, or lifting them down, is difficult for you, make yourself a Long-arm Tommy, as it is popularly called. This is merely hanging a *small* watering can (so that it is not very heavy to lift when full of water) on a hook at the end of a pole, plus a piece of string tied to the spout of the can and taken back to the holding end of the pole. Then, just lift into position and pull the string to tip the can.

CAULIFLOWERS

Many people find that cauliflowers are not the easiest of vegetables to grow satisfactorily. The reason for this is usually that they do not have sufficiently enriched moisture-retaining soil. It is, therefore, necessary to do all you can to improve the quality of your soil in these respects. Having done that, try this new method this year. In effect, it merely means growing your cauliflowers in a shallow trench.

Remove the top 5 or 6 inches of soil along the row, placing it on the windward side as the protection it affords the young plants is beneficial. Then set the plants in the trench, about 18 ins. apart, as shown in inset A.

The great advantage of this method is that as the plants grow they can be top-dressed every two or three weeks with an inch or so of a suitably rich mixture. This can easily be made up of equal parts of good top soil and sifted manure, if you can get it. If you can't get the manure, use well-rotted compost or, perhaps, one of the proprietary manures which come in a form suitable for immediate use without sifting.

In dry weather the plants should be well-watered, preferably with rain-water out of a butt, before applying the top-dressing. Eventually, of course, the dressing will fill the trench but by that time the cauliflowers should be growing strongly and making nice curds. When they have done so, the leaves will be large enough to break the main rib of one or two and bend down over the curds to protect them from the direct rays of the sun as these tend to discolour the curds. But don't be tempted to avoid having to do this by planting in a shady area. They need a sunny site as well as needing the shade provided by a leaf or two.

If you have grown and lifted early potatoes, that site is a good one for the cauliflowers. But before putting them in give the trench a dressing of superphosphate at 2 oz. per square yard, after you have taken out the top soil, of course. And keep the soil around the plants nicely moist at all times as they will not do well if suffering from thirst on hot, dry soil.

ROSE CARE

As everyone appreciates the beauty of roses in the garden or the home, it is well worthwhile to do all we can to improve and prolong the display.

The major step in this direction is to combat the pests and diseases which none of us can totally avoid. Nowadays, this is much easier, from the point of view of the work involved, than it used to be. The pests can be most effectively controlled by using a systemic insecticide and we can now combat the diseases, such as mildew and black spot, by using a systemic fungicide, called Benlate. Moreover, the two can be mixed together so that we need spray only once for a complete control. But you may have to do so at intervals, using your discretion after examining your rose trees, as the scientists haven't yet succeeded in discovering a product that lasts all season long.

Where black spot is concerned, illustrated in inset B, it is as well to pick off any badly affected leaves and to pick up any such leaves that have fallen off the bushes and *burn* them as if they are left lying on the ground they will spread the disease.

Another good practice is to feed your roses with a rose fertiliser. Apply it according to directions on container and water it in if the rain doesn't do the job for you.

Keep your rose beds free of weeds by hand weeding, not by hoeing. More harm is done to the roots of rose trees by hoeing than is generally realised. And it is this type of damage to the roots that is the most common cause of suckers arising from the stock on which the named variety has been budded.

If you are bothered by suckers, and it *is* important that they are removed, otherwise the vigour of the stock will seriously weaken the growth of the part of the plant you want to flower well, remove these suckers by *pulling* them off if you can. Scrape the soil away from the area where the sucker originates, preferably with the fingers so as not to do further damage, and pull the sucker away from the bush centre. If you cannot get it off without uprooting the plant, then cut it off, right at its point of origin and replace soil, pressing it down with a foot.

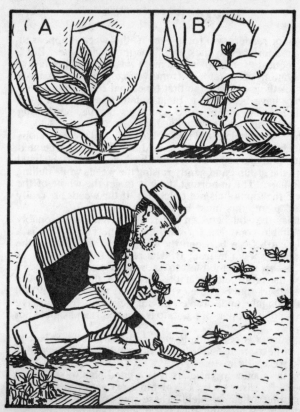

BEANS

Beans of one kind or another are a very important crop for most people. And of the beans, runners are the most popular. This is the week when runner bean plants raised under glass are put out—provided all risk of frost has gone. Being a native of tropical America, it will not stand the slightest frost.

Even if you haven't raised your own plants you can usually buy them quite easily at this time of year. Give them ground that has been deeply dug with rotted manure incorporated in the lower spit if you can—the experts prepare a special trench in this way for their runners, knowing that they like a deep root run and are a crop that must never be allowed to get thirsty. Peat incorporated into soil that is at all light is, therefore, very beneficial as it has great moisture retaining properties.

When putting out the plants in this way you must, of course, place them according to the arrangements you intend to make for their support, whether this is to be netting or the popular tent like arrangement of canes, etc. My standard planting plan is two double rows about 5 ft. apart, the plants being 9 in. apart in the rows. Each plant is then given its own support, the two rows of canes being brought together at the top.

Even if you put out plants in this way, why not sow the seed now of another row or two to ensure cropping succession? These rows you might try in the bush form, without supports. To make the plants "bush", nip out the growth points (see inset B) in due course.

And speaking of nipping out, make sure you remove the tops of your broad bean plants as soon as these are in flower (see inset A). This helps greatly to reduce black-fly trouble on this crop. If you are still bothered by black-fly lower down puff Malathion dust over the plants.

Having mentioned, "bush" runners, did you know you can go to the other extreme and grow climbing French beans? They reach about 4 ft. in height and need the same cultivation as runners. The seed can be sown now. And French beans, you know, produce a heavier yield per sq. yd. than runners!

POTATOES

I trust my more senior readers will forgive me if, this week, I appear to be "teaching my grandmother to suck eggs", as the saying goes. But I receive so many requests for help in the more basic gardening tasks, such as the cultivation of potatoes, from young people who have acquired a garden of their own for the first time, that I feel I must help them. Usually, they have been told to plant potatoes, as this is a good method of breaking up the uncultivated soil. This is true, but having planted potatoes, they do not know what to do next.

If, as I hope, they did not plant the tubers too early and the green tops have not been caught by a late frost, all should be well so far. The next step probably is to remove weeds. This should be done carefully by hand pushing a fork into the ground and gently raising the weeds while pulling them out with the hand. The important thing is to get the whole of the root out, pulling off the top only is not much use. If the weeds are really close to the potato plant, this must be done very carefully.

Having done this, the soil between the rows should be reasonably loose and in a suitable condition for earthing up the rows. This is a process of pulling earth from between the rows up to the neck of the plants, with the result shown in inset B. The reason for doing this, as shown in inset A, is that the plant if left to its own devices will produce a fair proportion of the crop quite near the surface of the ground. Any tubers or parts of tubers that become exposed to the air in this way will turn green. This is highly undesirable, as our scientific friends have proved that a green potato or part of a potato is poisonous and should not be eaten.

This surfacing process is not so likely with early varieties as it is with late ones as the earliest are usually dug in July and August for eating before the plants are really mature.

Before earthing up maincrop varieties it is a good plan to sprinkle a handful of a general fertiliser such as Growmore per yard run along the rows to ensure getting a heavier yield. These rows can be earthed up more than once during the growing season if it appears to be necessary.

SPRAYING POTATOES

As potatoes are such an important part of the staple diet of most families (those that are not dieting, anyway) we must take all necessary steps to ensure that the yield is not reduced by disease or pests.

Potato blight usually appears at the end of this month or early next, depending on the weather conditions at the time. It can be recognised by dark brown or almost black patches on the leaves, as shown in inset A, usually on the underside. It is a fungus disease and often quickly spreads, unless promptly dealt with, to the whole of the haulm, causing it to wither and even to the tubers at a later stage, producing soft, brown decayed patches in the flesh of the crop.

As soon as any sign of the disease is seen spray with a copper-based fungicide such as Bordeaux mixture, thoroughly wetting the foliage, particularly the underside as shown in inset B. In fact, if you have been troubled with this disease in the past, or if you know it is prevalent in your area, spray now anyway, whether you have seen it or not, as prevention is better than cure. In seriously affected areas it is wise to spray again three weeks after the first application.

At this time of year it is also wise to protect all your green crops such as cabbages, cauliflowers, Brussels sprouts and peas by spraying with an insecticide to put paid to all those horrible caterpillars, whitefly, thrips, etc., that do so much damage to such crops. Spray again if you see any evidence of such pests, even once a week is not too often to ensure completely pest-free results.

The same procedure should be followed for bush and cane fruits to avoid maggot infested fruit.

Many people spray their roses against green-fly but fail to realise that aphides of various kinds appear on many other subjects and unless these are also included in the spraying programme, the roses or other plants they have dealt with will be quickly re-infested from the unsprayed ones. Honeysuckle, for example, is often covered with aphides but how many people think of spraying that, or even look to see if it is infested? Treatment must be complete to be effective.

SUCCULENT CUTTINGS

Succulent cuttings can consist of off-shoots, leaves, or parts of stems. Carefully remove, with a sharp knife, the portions you propose to use and lay them aside on a shelf in a dry, warm place until a corky kind of skin has formed over the cut surface. This helps to prevent them rotting before they root.

I prefer to give each cutting a pot on its own—a 3 in. one is a suitable size. Three-quarters of each pot should contain a suitable potting compost. This is covered with the rooting medium so that the plant can produce its roots in this and then grow down into the richer compost below.

For most of these plants, John Innes No. 1 is suitable, provided its drainage properties are increased by mixing into it one sixth, by bulk, of coarse grit; the so-called river or washed grit is best. There are exceptions, such as the epiphyllums, which need the richer J.I. No. 2, plus the grit. One of these is shown in inset A and this is one easily propagated by cuttings.

The rooting medium to go into the top of the pot is a mixture of equal parts of peat and coarse grit. This is then lightly watered and allowed to drain for, say, one hour. The cuttings are then *placed* on top of the rooting medium. Note that I say *placed*—they should not be pushed into it. More cuttings rot, rather than root, because they have been embedded in the medium than for any other reason. If the cuttings are tall, support them on a little stick, so that the bottom just touches the sand and peat.

Put the pots in a sunny place and spray lightly occasionally if they really need it.

This brings me to the question of watering succulent plants. Care must be exercised—particularly with such popular ones as the rat-tailed cactus shown in inset B—which really means, if the compost is sufficiently porous, keeping it nicely moist at all times. Never dry and never wet.

DIANTHUS PROPAGATION

As soon as the various members of the Dianthus family—carnations and pinks—have finished flowering they can be increased by cuttings, pipings and layers.

Cuttings should be taken from the centre of the plant. Clear an inch or two of the stem of leaves, as shown in inset A, and insert the cuttings as far as the lowest leaf in very sandy soil, preferably in a shaded cold-frame. If you haven't a frame, try them in a shaded part of the garden but the soil must be sandy and well drained. A little V-shaped trench filled with sand would be quite suitable.

With pinks, you can try some cuttings but you are more likely to be successful if you use what we call pipings. These are the equivalent of cuttings but are not cut off. They are the centre part of a shoot actually pulled out. Hold the plant down with one hand and pull out the centre of a growing shoot. You'll find it will come out quite easily, giving you a nice clean new shoot ready for planting in the way described above.

For carnations, layering is usually more successful than taking cuttings. Cover the soil all round the plant with sand. Then lift a long shoot on the outside of the plant and cut partly through the second joint below the leaves so that a tongue is formed. Peg the stem down into the ground on the plant side of the cut joint and keep the tongue open by placing a small stick beside the rest of the shoot, as shown in inset B. Press some of the sand over the stem at this point and keep it moist.

In a few weeks, roots should have formed. You can usually tell by new fresh green leaves appearing in the centre of the shoot. The stem joining the shoot to the parent plant can then be cut. Leave for a week or two for the young plant to recover from the operation and then transfer it to a 3 in. pot.

Grow on in the pot in cold-frame or cool greenhouse for this winter and plant out in the garden again the following spring. You can plant out in the garden in the autumn if you wish but much better plants will result from the former method.

SWEDES

The Swede is a vegetable that is a very useful stand-by in the kitchen in the winter, provided its taste is to your liking. For some reason it has acquired a reputation for being rather gross, fit only for feeding to cattle rather than humans! In my opinion, nothing could be further from the truth. When properly cooked and mashed, I think it has a very distinctive flavour that is very welcome. For this reason I believe it should be much more widely grown, although some of those who have tried to grow it in the past have not been very successful, the roots having failed to develop into the globes we need for cooking. The reason for this has perplexed many gardeners for years because Swedes grown in farmers' fields do not seem to have this tendency. It almost seems as if they do better when grown together in large numbers.

I have found that delaying sowing Swedes in the garden until the first week of July is the best answer to the problem so far discovered. This has an additional advantage in general garden management as they can then occupy ground earlier used for another crop. This also suits the Swedes as they prefer an area manured well in advance. If the ground has not been limed this year give it a lime dressing (about 4 oz. to the square yard) before making the drill for the seed, which should be about ½ in. deep, rows 1 ft. apart. Sow thinly as the seedlings will have to be thinned until they are about 1 ft. apart in the row.

Swedes take about six months to mature but are quite hardy and can be in the ground until required for use. If you prefer to lift them, to avoid the need for trying to get them out of frozen ground, you can do so and store them in the same way as other root crops. Inset B shows a good variety to use, called Chignecto, that is resistant to club-root disease which is a problem in some areas as the Swede is a member of the cabbage (Brassica) family.

Inset A shows a good way to prevent slug damage. Just spread bonfire ash on the surface of the soil after sowing. Its potash content will later benefit the plants, while the gritty ash acts as a deterrent to slugs.

JAPANESE AZALEAS

Japanese Azaleas should be much more widely grown.

Don't be misled that azaleas are now classified as rhododendrons. It is under this heading that you now find them in many catalogues.

Azaleas can be broadly divided into two types. The first (in inset B) is the deciduous (leaf-losing) type. These have larger flowers than the others, but fewer of them and are slightly later in flowering. Their flowers are scented and range from white and yellow to orange and scarlet. These plants are also colourful in the autumn as their leaves assume very attractive reddish hues before they fall. They also grow to 5 or 6 ft. which is about twice the height of the other type, the so-called Japanese evergreen or miniature azalea (shown in inset A). As these keep their leaves as a rule—some do assume autumnal hints and fall—they are attractive all the year round. The leaves are very tiny and almost out of sight when the plants are in flower as the whole bush is smothered with hundreds of tiny blooms in one striking mass, often twice as wide as the plant is tall. For this reason one can wisely grow, here and there, one of the taller deciduous ones among the lower-growing kind to prolong the floral display.

You need lime-free soil with plenty of peat mixed in. If you feel your soil will still be too limy, use Sequestrene on it.

These shrubs also make splendid specimens to grow in pots or tubs but you must keep them well-watered.

They are frequently supplied in containers nowadays so they can be planted at any time, one need not wait until October as one did in the old days.

Few plants give such a brilliant display for so little attention. They normally need no pruning or any other attention. They do not seem to be prone to pests or diseases either. An annual mulch of peat is beneficial and the dead flowers can wisely be removed to prevent the formation of seed-pods, thus conserving the plant's energy for the production of next year's flowers, but that is all.

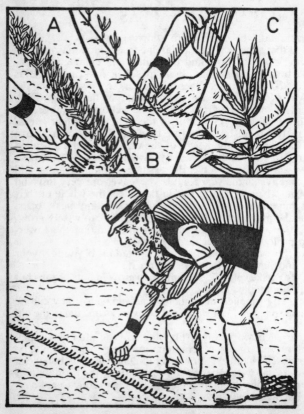

WALLFLOWERS

For a fine display of wallflowers, as a background to bulbs, for example, next spring, it is essential to sow the seed immediately. It is sown in a shallow drill, about ½ in. deep, in a seed-bed out-of-doors, making sure that the soil is really fine and nicely moist, watering it the previous day if necessary to ensure the correct conditions.

When the seedlings are 2 or 3 in. high they should be transplanted about 6 in. apart so that each plant can make sturdy, bushy growth. This bushiness is promoted by nipping out the top of each plant after they can be seen to be well established in their new positions. Keep the plants well watered if necessary as they must not be allowed to suffer from thirst as otherwise they suffer a check in growth which is difficult to remedy.

As soon as they are large enough and the ground is available, transfer them to their flowering positions. This should be done in October or November, the earlier the better, so that they have as long a period as possible, while the ground is still warm, to develop a good root system. Wallflowers are not really fussy about soil but they do appreciate land that is adequately limy, so give a dressing of lime before planting out, if the ground needs it.

There is more variety available in wallflowers than many people realise. Apart from old favourites, such as Fire King (scarlet) and Orange Bedder, we can get Ivory White, Purple Queen, etc., or a mixture of all the colours. Then there are giant flowered ones in similar colours. All these are about 18 in. high. The dwarf varieties, 9 in. high, come in similar colours and mixed, while a strain called Persian Carpet is a wonderful blend of pastel shades of all the usual colours. There's even an early-flowering strain (3 weeks early) that grows 2 ft. high and is specially bred for cutting.

We should also not overlook Siberian Wallflowers (Cheiranthus), grown in the same way, which form sweetly-scented successors to the others in orange-yellow, only 12 in. high and also suitable for a rockery. Which reminds me that we also have the alpine wallflower, 9 in. high, which has violet-mauve flowers.

LETTUCES FOR WINTER

YOU WOULD not need to be an economist to predict that food is unlikely to become cheaper.

So why not take an inflation beating tip from me and grow some lettuces yourself—right now.

For the price you paid for a couple of lettuces in summer, I can show you how to raise lettuces to enjoy between late autumn and early summer next year.

Think of the saving: Your home-grown lettuces will be ready when the shop lettuces are at their most expensive.

In addition to the dozens of salads, with a multitude of ingredients, you can use lettuce in many other tasty ways.

For instance, braised lettuce in meat stock, a classic French way of preparing lettuce as a vegetable for main dishes. With its official French title, it sounds rather posh: *Laitues braisées au gras.*

Lettuce leaves, too, can be seasoned with oil, lemon juice, pepper and salt, dipped in a light batter and deeply fried. This dish—*Laitues en fritôt,* as it is called—when served, garnished with parsley, looks and tastes marvellous.

And what about some piping hot "peppery" *potage crème de laitues*—cream of lettuce soup—on a bleak winter's day?

If the French are the experts making salads with their vinaigrette dressings, and cooking the lettuces, we British could give them a few tips on growing them.

There are almost as many varieties of lettuce available to sow at this time of year as there are for the spring.

Lettuces require a fertile, well-drained soil which contains a fair amount of organic matter. It is the lack of this final ingredient which causes many summer lettuces to be heart-less and to bolt—that is, run to seed.

Lettuces can follow any crop. So you do not have to worry about crop rotation.

Here is how to get your soil ready for sowing: Fork over the ground lightly and give it a dressing of *well-rotted* garden compost (NOT farmyard manure) or moistened peat and 2oz. of granular general fertiliser to each square yard. Finally tread the ground firm and lightly rake the bed level.

The seeds should be sown as thinly as possible in drills ½in. deep, lightly covered with soil and carefully watered. The length and position of the drills do not matter as the lettuce seedlings will have to be transplanted later.

If like me you are troubled by woodpigeons, sparrows, and possibly even rabbits, I would suggest covering the seed bed with inexpensive plastic netting supported a few inches from the soil on stakes. With rabbits, you may need a similar arrangement but using wire netting.

Lettuces sown outdoors in mid September should germinate in six to twelve days. Strangely enough you will get better results then than you do during the hotter days of summer. For too high soil temperatures cause germination failures.

Again, depending on the weather, I would expect lettuces

sown outdoors in Southern England to be ready for transplanting from 6 to 9 in. apart in late October and to be ready to use from winter to early summer.

I would like to be more specific, but I honestly do not know whether or not we are in for a mild or a severe winter. But one thing is certain: the lettuces will stand up to the worst that winter has to offer.

In northern areas, depending on the seedlings' growth, transplanting may have to be postponed until next February. But you will still have a superb crop of lettuces at a time when they are very expensive in the shops.

If you want more predictable results, anywhere in the country, the answer is to grow some of your crop in a greenhouse or cold frame.

There is a wonderful group of cabbage lettuces in the K series—Kordaat, Kweik, Kloek and Knap—which have been specially bred to produce a succession of excellent lettuces under glass from November to April, and with the exception of Kordaat, you do not need heat in your greenhouse.

Three other cabbage lettuces worth considering for planting under glass are: Emerald, May Queen and Premier.

Outdoors you can sow Imperial Winter, Arctic King and Valdor. The last named, although the seed is "expensive" is my particular choice because of its consistently good results over the winter. In fact this one variety can keep you supplied with lettuces from four to five months.

If you are short of space—you may only have a window box or balcony or a few tubs on a courtyard—I also strongly recommend Winter Density which is a dwarf and compact

cos lettuce. It needs to be thinned to a mere 6in. apart and from a packet of seeds you will be amazed at the number and quality of plants you can produce.

Even winter lettuces suffer from pests. So protect your outdoor lettuces from root damage with Root Guard at the time of transplanting, or by watering the soil with liquid malathion. Slugs can be kept away with slug pellets.

Indoors in badly ventilated greenhouses, grey mould which causes plants to collapse and die may be a problem. The solution is to spray regularly with systemic fungicide.

The lettuce has come a long way from its humble origins as a wild plant in Europe.

It is really the Romans you have to thank for its being adopted as a garden vegetable. The word lettuce itself comes from the Latin *lactuca,* because when a lettuce is cut it exudes a milky sap.

Lettuces were once served at the end of a Roman evening meal, because it was believed that after such a dessert one would sleep better. This belief was, I suspect, borne out in practice. For certain wild lettuces do contain a narcotic which would induce a restful sleep.

However, the Romans gradually adapted the lettuce as an appetiser and with the addition of several dressings they invented what nowadays we regard as *hors-d'oeuvre.*

Is it any wonder then that I regard the lettuce as a king among vegetables?

With slimming salads and so many tasty dishes, all for the price of a few seeds, can you think of any other vegetable or plant more worthy of a place in your garden in the coming autumn and winter?

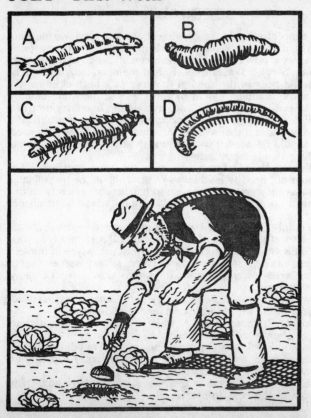

PEST CONTROL

The two pests which probably do most harm in the soil to the roots or stems of both flowers and vegetables, as well as in the lawn, are wireworms and leatherjackets, shown in insets A and B. You should learn to distinguish these from centipedes, shown in inset C. These also should be distinguished from millipedes, shown in inset D, as these are also harmful. Millipedes roll up into a ball when disturbed.

Where A, B, and D are present, mix BHC with the top soil, 1 oz. per square yard.

For wireworms, in particular, traps can be set. These are simply cut pieces of potato or carrot pushed on to a stick and buried in the top soil. The sticks show where they are and they should be taken up regularly and the catch destroyed. The pieces of vegetable will need renewing from time to time as they dry out. It is best not to grow root crops in ground known to be infested by this pest for two seasons. In that time the BHC and traps should have cleared up the trouble.

BHC is also good for several other pests such as ants, woodlice, earwigs, etc. As a spray, BHC is also useful against aphis and leaf-miner. The latter chiefly attacks the leaves of chrysanthemums and both sides of the leaves should be sprayed. This spray can also be used against cuckoo-spit but it must be applied very forcefully as you have to penetrate the froth with which the creature surrounds itself.

Where ants are particularly troublesome, you may well need to use a special ant-killer, but I have found a kettle of boiling water as effective as anything for these pests.

The special pellets sold for getting rid of slugs are also effective against snails.

One golden rule as a preventive measure against pests in general is to clear up all rubbish. Waste foliage left lying about is a heaven-sent haven for them, which doesn't mean you cannot have a compost heap. When properly constructed, such a heap engenders sufficient heat that pests are destroyed or they do not congregate there.

BIENNIALS

While we are concentrating on the growing of our own food, we must not neglect opportunities of growing our own flowers. For this reason, I advocate the sowing now of seeds of the biennials, such as Canterbury Bells, Brompton Stocks, Wallflowers, Forget-me-nots, etc., that will be planted out in the beds in the autumn to serve as a back-cloth for the spring bulbs as both should bloom more or less at the same time.

You need a seed-bed in a good site, away from overhanging trees, where the soil can be lightly forked and raked down to a fine tilth. If it seems rather dry, water it thoroughly overnight, before sowing the seed. No fertiliser should be needed with ground in good heart as we do not want to produce rapid, sappy growth.

Make shallow drills as shown and sow the seed sparingly. The seedlings should not need to be thinned out but should be transplanted singly as soon as they are large enough to handle conveniently so that each grows into a sturdy bushy plant by planting-out time—September or early October.

There are a number of improved varieties in most catalogues to choose from so make a careful selection of those that appeal particularly to you.

Our insets show three suggestions. A is Verbascum, a type of mullein, which can be obtained as yellow flowers on silvery spikes (Arctic Summer) or as large-flowered hybrids in various shades from creamy-white to rose-mauve.

In inset B we show a cup-and-saucer variety of Canterbury Bell which ranges in colour from white to pink, lavender and blue.

C shows double Brompton Stocks, which include all the Canterbury Bell colours of slightly different shades.

When Brompton Stock seedlings are being planted out discard all the dark-green-leaved ones, as they produce single flowers. Keep only the *light*-green ones, as they are the doubles.

In colder districts Brompton Stocks are best wintered in a cold-frame and planted out in the beds in March.

PARSLEY

Parsley is a herb that is often required in the kitchen in winter and spring, when there isn't any in the garden. This need can be overcome by sowing some now. You don't even need a space in the vegetable plot for it—you can use it as an edging to the flower border as its foliage makes it a very attractive plant.

. If the border has had manure or compost dug in already this is ideal as parsley likes rich, deeply cultivated soil. Just rake the surface fine and smooth and sow thinly half-an-inch deep.

The seed is one of the slowest to germinate, often taking five or six weeks before appearing. This process can often be speeded up by soaking the seed in warm water for 24 hours before sowing.

When the seedlings are large enough to handle comfortably, thin them out to 6 in. apart (see inset). Given sufficient space in this way to develop fully, they will make nice bushy little plants forming a pleasing edging and at the same time producing plenty of the foliage so useful as a garnish and as flavouring for various dishes.

Few people seem to know that the stalks, chopped up, add a pungent flavour to fish, meat and sauces. In the second year, the roots also can be used, chopped up or grated, to add a parsnip-like flavour to such dishes.

There are several outstanding varieties of parsley on the market now. For flavour, one called French is recommended, while a newer one called Green Velvet, which has great cropping potential, is considered better than Moss Curled which we all used to grow. The variety which probably stands the winter better than any other is Asmer New Dark Green Winter. Also winter-resistant is a new variety called Bravour. This one, like another called King of the Parsleys (a very dwarf kind), is specially recommended for those people who wish to store some for future use in their deep freeze.

A small packet, costing a few pences, is quite sufficient for most families as it will sow a row 30 ft. long.

FLOWER STAKING

Although I am sure most people appreciate that many of the plants that give the finest displays of flowers in the garden need supports, all too often damage is done by wind before suitable action is taken, or the supporting is done in the wrong way.

Ruined plants can easily be avoided if a few simple rules are observed.

Never tie plants tightly round the middle to just one support, as shown in insets A and B. Don't give tall plants stakes that are too short, so that the top of the plant flops over or is broken off by the wind above the support. Similarly, don't put tall stakes to short plants, they look so unsightly.

Always put the stakes in fairly early, so that the plant grows around them and thus hides them, as an upright, apparently unsupported plant looks so much more effective. With bushy subjects such as delphiniums or dahlias place three or four stakes round each plant, each sloping slightly outward so that the upper part of the plant—the important part from the floral display aspect—is not crushed together in a mass of foliage. The plant will then flower better and will look more natural.

When securing plants with single woody stems to supports, such as standard roses or young fruit trees, it is very important that the tie or the stake does not chafe the plant stem. Special ties can, of course, be brought for this purpose but one of the best ways I have found is to use an old piece of hose in the way shown in inset C. It is surprising how many gardeners have a length of old hose lying around not being used. Simply cut off a short piece of the hose for each tie, thread the string through it, and fix it round the plant stem as shown, securing it in a position which prevents any possibility of chafing when the wind blows.

It is also very important to use stakes sufficiently strong to withstand the strongest winds in the autumn. This is particularly true with dahlias as I have found that we always seem to get a gale for a day or two when dahlias are carrying their greatest loads of blooms with disastrous results if the stakes are not strong enough. I confess that I have had dahlia plants broken off at ground level and blown completely flat.

TOMATO CARE

Although the successful growing of tomatoes out of doors in this country depends to a great extent on the weather during the summer we can do quite a lot to assist the plants to overcome adverse conditions. If, as I hope, you are growing yours against a fence or some other screen from which they will benefit by protection from the wind and by the reflected warmth, you have taken the first important step. It must be realised, however, that such a screen may also protect them from some of the rain and they may, therefore, need more watering to keep them nicely moist *at all times.* This is really essential. They must *not* alternate between wet and dry. If they do, you are almost certain later on to have troubles, such as fruit with split skins or badly shaped.

Another "must" is the regular and early removal of all side-shoots (inset A) that grow from the leaf axils on the main stem or even direct from the bottom of the plants at ground level. If you find a leaf shoot developing at the end of a flower truss after the fruit has set, nip that out as well.

Once the tiny green fruit can be seen on the lowest flower truss, you can start feeding the plant (inset B). It should not be done earlier, as then you get too much growth of stem between the fruit trusses.

As with watering, here again regular and correct quantity application is very important. Follow exactly the directions on the container of the feed you use. A stop-go, haphazard policy is, if anything, worse than not feeding at all.

When you have three (or, perhaps, four in some favoured district or a particularly good summer) trusses of fruit set, nip out the top of the plant to concentrate the plant's energy into maturing that quantity of fruit. You, also, should emulate the plant and concentrate on maturing that quantity of fruit unless you are quite happy to have a lot of green tomatoes remaining at the end of the season that you propose to use for making green tomato chutney.

The plant may well try to rebel against this concentration effort by rapidly sending out vigorous side-shoots. These must be removed.

Young shoot

sand

grit, peat, leaf-mould

PRUNING HYDRANGEAS

The best period in which to prune hydrangeas is shortly after they have completed blooming and the flower heads have faded. Cut these off with two or three pairs of leaves below them.

The length of shoot when pruning is determined by the need to keep the bush in a good shape.

Also remove weak shoots. From among the strong shoots which have not flowered choose some for use as cuttings, but do not take too many from any one shrub as these non-flowering shoots will bear next season's blooms.

Make a cut just below a node or joint after taking off the lower leaves. Have some 2½ in. and 3½ in. pots ready filled with sandy soil or vermiculite, the smaller pots to take single cuttings and the larger to hold three inserted round the edge.

Before planting put silver sand into each planting hole. After watering them put the pots into a glass-covered box in the greenhouse or in a shaded part of the garden.

Syringe the cuttings with tepid water on sunny days, keeping them protected from strong sunlight. Admit air daily for a time.

When roots have formed pot them singly, using a compost of equal parts of leaf-mould, peat, and grit. Avoid lime in the compost used for blue-flowered kinds.

Although you don't prune these "hortensia" hydrangeas severely, you can cut out the really old branches if necessary. If the shrubs are in an exposed position you can also leave the dead flower heads on until the spring to give protection from frost to next year's buds.

If a bush has become very straggly and out-of-hand or has overgrown its position, cut back all the growth, apart from any from ground level produced this year. This is drastic treatment but you'll find that the bush will respond very well providing it is growing in soil that is reasonably rich and moist. The strong new growth can then be used as the basis for a nice, shapely bush that you can keep properly trimmed in future.

SUMMER WATERING

Seldom does a year go by nowadays when we are not urged during the summer to use as little water as possible.

There are several ways in which we can do this. The most obvious way, of course, is to instal a butt to catch the rain-water from a garage, conservatory, greenhouse, etc.

Water kept in this way will have its temperature raised by the sun and will thus be more suitable for watering plants than water straight from mains, which is really too cold.

The chemical treatment of mains water also makes it unsuitable for use on certain plants, such as azaleas, rhododendrons, etc., in fact, all plants that dislike lime. Rain-water from a butt should not be used in a greenhouse as it may have picked up from the roof bacteria, etc., which could introduce diseases into the house which were not there before.

If your soil is caked hard before watering spike around the plants to a depth of 3 or 4 inches, as shown in inset A, so that the water you apply gets down to the roots. Wetting the surface of the soil is unimportant, down below the plant is where the moisture needs to be. In fact, wetting only the surface can be definitely harmful as it may induce the plant's roots to come up for the water where they will die from thirst as soon as the surface dries out again.

By far the best plan is to mulch the surface of the ground while it is still moist, thus preventing it drying out and making it unnecessary to water at all. This not only saves water, it saves labour as well.

Any vegetable matter can be used as a mulch, except grass-cuttings from a weed-killer treated lawn. Even piles of weeds (which we do *not* seem to be running short of) can be used, provided they were uprooted before they went to seed, as they should have been.

Keep the mulch away from plant stems—*don't* pile it up as shown in inset B. In the autumn this mulch can be dug into the ground to improve its texture, in both light and heavy ground, thus it will be of double benefit.

IRISES

One of my favourite flowers is the tall bearded iris, commonly called, with a rather derogatory air, the old English flag. Its origin, the common blue flag, iris germanica, was, perhaps, so frequently seen in cottage gardens as not to be very highly prized. But how different the scene now, with over 300 different named varieties to choose from!

Where clumps are in need of lifting and dividing to rejuvenate them or to increase stock, now is the time to do it. It is also the time to plant new ones for those who haven't yet joined the iris growers fraternity.

This is one of the few flowers that is best replanted soon after flowering as by doing it now, the rhizomes, as the fleshy root-stocks are called, have every opportunity of making new roots in the warm soil and thus can really establish themselves before the winter sets in.

Lift a clump with a fork carefully as shown. Shake off the soil and divide it up so that you have a good-sized portion of rhizome with roots and leaves attached, as shown in inset A, for each replanting. These are usually the outside parts, the old centre being discarded. Cut off the top third of the leaves, but don't overdo this as it is only intended to reduce wind resistance until the plant is established.

If you have a limy soil, irises are for you, as this is what they prefer. Choose a sunny, well-drained spot. If the ground is on the wet, heavy side, raise the area an inch or so above the general level. If the soil is light, work in some compost or peat to increase its ability to retain moisture, but don't use manure as this will only cause excessive leaf growth, at the expense of flowers:

If your ground needs lime, give a dressing before planting. It would also be an advantage in any soil to add a sprinkling of bonfire ash or bone-meal and mix this in.

Plant each piece so that the roots can go down as far as they need, but keep the rhizome on the surface of the soil as it likes to be warmed by the sun. Plant it too deeply and you'll probably find it will not flower the following year.

DO-IT-YOURSELF FLOWERS

As most gardeners are all too well aware, our hobby is very much a do-it-yourself activity—unless, like me, you have a very co-operative wife! This is a field where women's lib is unnecessary as, in many cases, the ladies are just as keen gardeners as the men.

Help, however, can also be obtained from do-it-yourself plants, as I call them. These are the ones, in the main, that do our seed sowing and plant production for us.

One of the best in this respect is the old favourite, now produced in some splendid modern forms, the fox-glove. If allowed to go to seed, and it doesn't harm the plant to allow it to do this, it will seed itself very freely. It is particularly useful in this way in a shrubbery. At a time, usually in June, when the azaleas, rhododendrons, etc., are mostly over, the fox-glove comes into its own, producing some splendid spikes of flowers in all sorts of odd corners, giving the shrubbery a real, old-world charm.

Some of the newer fox-gloves are called Excelsior Hybrids, which range in colour from white and pale yellow to deep pink, many with darker spots in the throat. There's also a dwarf kind, Foxy mixed.

Then what about the forget-me-not? You probably know this is a self-sower. It can be obtained in at least three shades of blue as well as a rosy pink.

Honesty is another of our do-it-yourself friends. There are several forms, white, pink, lilac and purple, although the flowers are not particularly impressive. Its real value is in the seed-pods themselves (see inset) which eventually look like silver pennies, are "everlasting", and are much-prized for indoor winter decorative flower arrangements.

Also in this class can be included the herb, borage, which has blue flowers and whose leaves can be used in cooking to impart a cucumber-like flavour.

Evening primrose is another useful plant in this respect—and there's even a white one that remains open all day, as well as the more common yellow forms.

SUMMER PRUNING

This is the month for the summer pruning of pears and apples—in that order. The end of the month is usually the best time for apples, with pears coming about a week earlier.

This question of summer pruning is one on which the specialists appear to be equally divided—for and against—as far as normal types of tree are concerned, such as bush or standard. But all agree that it should be done where specially trained trees, such as cordons or espaliers are concerned.

The first question for the home gardener to answer is—for what purpose is he going to prune? If you have young trees—that is, under 5 years old—you should be mainly concerned with building up a good, basic, branch formation, so that you have a balanced head, nicely open in the centre, like a wine glass on its stem, for example, in the case of a bush or standard tree.

The summer pruning of such a tree is confined to shortening *side*-shoots to 4 or 5 leaves, plus the removal of any spindly growth or even a vigorous shoot going in the wrong direction—across another towards the centre of the tree, for example. You do *not* touch the leading shoots in summer—that comes later, in winter.

Where cordons and espaliers are concerned, the side-shoots can be shortened a little further—to, say, 3 leaves. When making all these cuts, remove the end piece *just* above a leaf, as shown in inset A, *not* midway between leaves, as this is likely to cause die-back.

Another point that often confuses beginners is that they feel that a tree that is growing very vigorously, such as a Bramley Seedling, must be cut back much more than normal. This is the opposite of the truth. It should be pruned much more lightly than normal—in fact, keep the pruning of such a tree to the minimum, if you can, as the harder you prune, the more it will grow.

Another example of summer pruning we can wisely practise now is the shortening of the side growths of gooseberry bushes to keep them as open as possible.

PRUNING CANE FRUITS

As soon as the fruiting season is over for all the cane fruits, raspberries, blackberries, loganberries, etc., they should be pruned. (If you are growing autumn-fruiting raspberries this stage will not yet have been reached, of course.) As this process is probably the simplest pruning procedure in the gardener's calendar it is surprising how often one sees in gardens rows of neglected cane-fruits that are a mass of woody growth producing poor crops of small fruit simply because they have not been properly pruned or not pruned at all.

Pruning simply consists of cutting out, at ground level, all the growths produced before those of the current year. These are quite easily distinguished as the old ones are those that have fruited, and are darker in colour and more woody in texture.

Where the bushes are well-established and growing on good fertile land they may well have made more new growth this year than you need. Each bush should be allowed to retain four to six new canes, the rest being removed. Naturally, you choose the weaker or misshapen ones to cut out. Burn all the cut growth to destroy disease.

If you do not have sufficient good new canes arising directly from the ground but have some good new shoots originating near the base of older ones, these can be retained, cutting out the old wood just above the point where the new one starts.

The new canes should be nicely spaced along the supports in the row and tied in position (inset A) so that they ripen properly ready for a bumper crop next year. This makes care and fruit-picking so much easier later on.

These fruits have a habit of making a lot of small growths quite a way from the original root. These should be raised with a fork, preferably when the ground is moist, and removed. Many of these pieces can be planted out to increase your stock if you wish.

When all this has been done give the plants a good mulch of manure or compost, at least 3 inches deep, when the ground is moist (inset B). The response next year may well surprise you.

GROW YOUR OWN VINEYARD

IMAGINE IF you had a garden in the South of France where the landscape is dotted with pencil-slim cypresses and white-washed buildings. Where the air is heavy with the scent of orange and lemon blossom in spring and the fragrance of lavender fields in summer.

Just the sort of ideal climate for growing the odd vine or two to produce some fresh dessert grapes for the table.

Yet did you know that you can grow just as good grapes for eating back in Britain?

Vines will grow in any well-drained soil, including chalk and clay, in a position which gets plenty of sunshine. As well as growing grapes in the open you can also plant vines against house walls.

Outdoors it is best to choose varieties which ripen by late August or September.

For example, the following grapes, would be a good choice for dessert: Siegerrebe (gold berries), Precoce de Malingre (gold), Muscat Noir Hâtif de Marseille (dark red), Marshal Joffre (black) and Muscat de Saumur (gold).

These are French grapes, but you might like to try a couple of very early ripening Russian hybrids which give excellent results in Britain. They are Gagarin Blue (bluish black) and Tereshkova (purple-red with a muscat flavour).

These grapes are mainly for eating, but what if you want to try your hand at making your own wine?

I suggest the following reliable varieties. First for French-type red wine: Seibel 13053, with black grapes which are highly rated by viticulturists both in Britain and France, and Leon Millot (black). Now French-type white wine: Seyve-Villard 5276 (heavy crops which ripen every year). Next Alsatian or German hock-type wines: Madeleine Angevine 7672 (white), Madeleine Sylvaner 2851 (white) and Riesling Sylvaner (white).

Vines should be planted at 3 ft. intervals against a framework of wires, running preferably north/south, with 3ft. between subsequent rows. To make this framework you need two stout 4ft. long wooden fence posts at the end of each 10ft. row with one thick galvanised wire 1ft. from the ground and the other 2½ft. from the ground.

The soil should be forked over before planting and peat or compost worked in to lighten it. Finally you can give a dressing of 4oz. to the square yard of granular fertiliser.

After the vines have been planted they should be cut back to 6in. from the ground. Then a thick bamboo cane, about 5ft. long, should be stuck into the ground close to each vine and lashed to the wires.

In March give the row of vines a moisture-retaining and weed-suppressing mulch of farmyard manure, compost or peat. By about June the apparently dead vines will make lots of new growth. Three shoots should be allowed to flourish (cut away the others) and they should be carefully tied to the cane.

After leaf fall, the strongest two shoots should be removed from the cane, shortened to 2½ft. long and tied one on either side of the cane on the lower wire thus making a T-shape. The third shoot should be cut away at four buds from the ground.

The following summer the shoots tied to the lower wire will produce side-shoots which will quickly grow upwards to the upper wire where they should be secured with raffia.

The shoot which you cut down to the ground the previous autumn should be permitted to produce three new shoots. These should be tied to the cane and "topped" as before.

In late July or August it will be necessary to go along the top wire with hedging shears or secateurs clipping away excessive growth.

After leaf fall the shoots which have borne fruit are cut away completely and the three shoots on the cane are untied and given the same treatment as before.

If you have a south or west facing wall or fence, you can put two wires on that at the same height as with the vineyard and grow your grapes in exactly the same way. Alternatively you can have a vine much higher up on the wall.

In this instance you need a different growing technique: the first year only one shoot should be allowed to grow up and along a single thick wire.

In the autumn the single shoot should be trimmed back to 2in. beyond the ripened wood, which is reddish brown; immature wood is yellowish green and tends to go mouldy in winter: that's why it is cut back.

The following year the vine will sprout and continue to lengthen. It will also produce fruit-bearing side-shoots, which should be restricted to two from every bud on the main stem.

The fruit-bearing shoots should be cut off at the second leaf past the clusters of flowers, as soon as these have formed. After leaf fall, the shoots which bore fruit should be cut right back to two buds from the main stem. Don't be timid: use your shears.

With this system, you should limit the vine to one bunch of grapes for every 9in. of main stem. Even so, a 25ft.-long house wall can easily produce 48 bunches, weighing 30lb. to 40lb.

In Northern England and Scotland you can use this method of viticulture to grow grapes in a greenhouse. The vine is best planted outside and a single stem led inside after a pane of glass has been removed. The stem should be trained along the ridge and there should be a framework of wires in the eaves to secure the side-shoots.

With a greenhouse, you can also have the following late ripening dessert grapes, Muscat de Hambourg (black), Muscat St. Vallier (gold) and the Swiss hybrid Golden Chasselas, to produce fresh grapes for Christmas.

Fortnightly feeds in summer with a liquid general fertiliser are beneficial to outdoor and greenhouse vines too. Plenty of water is vital to prevent the fruit skins splitting.

Vines indoors too must not have heat in winter. Leave the greenhouse door and ventilators open to let the frost in and to ensure that the vine is rested properly, otherwise it will not fruit satisfactorily.

Wouldn't it be wonderful to eat your own grapes, or to be able to open a bottle of your very own wine for lunch?

BORDER FLOWERS TO PLANT

By this time of year most of us are viewing our flower borders with a fairly critical eye, noting spaces where improvements can be made, or rearrangement may appear necessary. Many of us, too, have spotted subjects in our friends' gardens that make us rather envious.

So I am going to suggest four flowers that you may not possess which can be ordered now for autumn planting.

The positions in the border can also be prepared now, but don't go digging in a lot of manure—it would be far better to give such material in the form of a mulch after the plants have been set in position.

Now, to give them in alphabetical order, there's an Artemisia which is grown for its splendid silvery-white plumes of foliage, 2 ft. high. As a backcloth to a deeply coloured flower spike, this is superb. I favour a variety called Augustifolia. You may say this is not strictly a flower but I can assure you in appearance it is just as effective as a flower—in many cases where flowers are massed the contrast is even more effective than more blossom would be. Far too little use is made of foliage plants in our gardens.

Next we come to Echinacea Purpurea, shown in inset A. The modern hybrids are really splendid having unique wine-coloured crimson flowers, 4-5 in. across, that are ideal for cutting. From the shape of the blooms you can see why it is popularly called the purple cone-flower. Three feet high.

Inset B shows my next suggestion—Sidalcea. Here again you want the modern hybrids which produce flowers in many shades of pink, lilac, etc., in shape very like the popular mallow, to which it is related. The plants grow about 3 ft. tall.

Now we come to Veronica—and what a beauty she is! Dainty spikes of masses of tiny flowers, pink or blue mainly. One is as tall as 3½ ft. (deep blue) while another is only 6 in. high (evergreen, pink, good for rock gardens). Another combines silvery foliage with violet flowers in spikes only 9 in. high.

CYCLAMEN

Those beautiful pots of Persian Cyclamen (C. Persicum) that many people are given as Christmas presents have always been among my favourite flowers. To me, their shapely blooms have all the elegance of a floral ballet.

Have you ever tried to grow your own? If you would like to try, now is the time to do so. Assuming you were successful, you would have a supply of inexpensively produced presents to give to your friends—but for the next Christmas, not this year!

You'll need a greenhouse later on, but the seed-box should be placed in a cold-frame first of all. I suggest you use a soil-less compost as I find that most successful. Fill a seedbox with it and water well. Leave to drain for a couple of hours before sowing the seed which is large enough to be sown singly and thus evenly spaced out, to avoid the need for pricking out. Cover the seed with a light layer of compost, not more than a quarter of an inch deep, place a sheet of glass on top and cover that with newspaper.

Don't be impatient as the seed is slow to germinate, seldom taking less than 4 or 5 weeks. When the seedlings have appeared remove paper and glass and when they are large enough to handle conveniently pot up singly. Later on transfer to larger pots and, of course, move these to the greenhouse when the weather turns cold. The variety shown in inset A, called Decora, gives a good range of pastel pink shades.

If you already have some corms from last year, now is the time to start them into growth again so that they are in flower by Christmas. Soak the soil in the pots thoroughly and when the plants are growing freely re-pot them so as to give them fresh nourishment. Liquid fertiliser should be given as soon as the buds appear.

Not all cyclamen need warmth. The hardy ones, such as Neapolitanum shown in inset B, can be planted now in a rockery, shrubbery or under trees. The flowers appear before the leaves which, being green streaked with silver, make a splendid backcloth for early spring flowers.

SPRING CABBAGE

This year especially every gardener with a vegetable plot should be paying special attention to the provision of fresh vegetables for use in the early part of next year. Despite government measures to combat inflation I feel sure that even higher prices will obtain in greengrocers' shops next spring.

One of the simplest ways of doing this is by growing spring cabbages. Sowing your own now is the cheapest way but even if you have to buy plants to put out later on the advantages are tremendous.

The first important consideration is the choosing of the varieties to grow and I suggest you grow more than one as some mature earlier than others. You thus get a longer period of supply for the kitchen. If you know that certain varieties do well in your area, choose those. If not, study your catalogues and choose those you think will best suit you.

Two good early ones are shown in the insets—A is April and B is Durham Early—but there are others, such as a new F1 hybrid called Hispi, which is ready earlier than other spring cabbages if over-wintered in a cold frame and planted out in early spring. Then there's First Early Market 218 which can be sown *in situ*, thinned out instead of being transplanted and should produce collards (spring greens) from January onwards. If left to mature it makes the largest heads in the shortest possible time.

Make your seed-bed in a spot where you can rake the surface down to a fine tilth. If it is dry soak the bed overnight and when you have sown the seed and covered it in spread a layer of well-moistened peat over the top to stop the surface drying out before the seed has germinated.

Plant out in late September or early October when the seedlings have made about 4 in. of growth. You'll probably have far more than you require so choose the best, the dark-green, sturdy ones, to plant out in ground manured for a previous crop. Don't use fertiliser on them as you don't want to produce soft, sappy growth that would not stand up well to the winter's frosts.

HEDGES

One often sees hedges that have been trimmed wrongly, while on other occasions one sees hedges that look so much more attractive because they have been dealt with in a really expert way.

As a general rule, it is wise—and less time-consuming—to clip a hedge when it has in the main finished its growth for the year. If you do it too early it will need doing again and if you leave it too late the growth will be more woody and harder to cut. This, as I say, is the general rule but some, such as privet, will need doing more than once.

The next important point is to choose the right tool for the job. Some old countrymen I know use a hook very expertly, covering a length of hedge in a surprisingly short time; but that is an acquired skill few gardeners possess.

For large-leaved hedges such as laurel, holly and bay, use secateurs or loppers, as shown in inset A, cutting each stem separately. This avoids cutting in half the large leaves, as one would with shears, as the remaining portions would turn brown and die, thus harming the hedge and making it look very unsightly.

With small-leaved hedges, such as privet, shears should be used but even better, if you can afford it, are the powered hedge trimmers as they save so much time, provided you do not have a lot of thick, hard woody stems to contend with. If you have, cut these out first with secateurs before using the trimmer.

The shape of the finished hedge is also important. It should be wider, or at least as wide, at the base as it is at the top. Inset B shows the wrong shape and C shows the correct one. These illustrations are purposely shown in a rather extreme form to depict clearly the principle involved.

A gap in a hedge can often be satisfactorily filled by driving a stake in the centre of the gap and tying to it branches from the bushes on each side. This lowering of the branches stimulates them into making extra growth along their length and thus effectively filling the gap in a comparatively short time.

SHRUB CUTTINGS

As well as introducing new shrubs for winter-flowering, we can increase our stock of shrubs we already have and admire, by taking cuttings now.

These are "taken", as we call it, in three main ways, as shown in the insets. The first, the woody ones, are pulled off with a "heel" attached; the second are the soft-wood ones, cut cleanly across immediately below a node, or joint; and finally special ones, like Clematis, which are cut across mid-way *between* two nodes.

The pieces to choose are those almost mature, produced during the current year, 6 to 8 in. long. Remove the lower leaves as shown, so that all the leaves left on will be above ground when the cuttings are planted.

The best results are usually obtained when they are inserted in a V-shaped trench in the open garden, in a shady spot, and covered with cloches, panes of glass arranged as an inverted V, or even with glass jam-jars.

The trench should be prepared beforehand as there should be as little loss of sap from the cuttings as possible before they are planted. Mix plenty of sand and peat or leaf-mould in the bottom of the trench so that the ends of the cuttings are imbedded in the mixture.

Dip the ends of the cuttings in water and then in a hormone-rooting powder before putting them in position. Fill in with medium soil and press quite firm. They must be kept moist under the coverings, watering if necessary.

Covering is not essential. You can root cuttings without it. But if you have some available use it as it increases your rooting chances. Don't expect every cutting you take to root—anything higher than 50 per cent and you are doing very well. So it pays to put in considerably more than you really need. If you have any excess they are never difficult to give away.

Most cuttings taken now should be rooted sufficiently for moving next spring. But don't be in too much hurry. If you are in any doubt leave them where they are until the following autumn. Not being moved won't do them any harm.

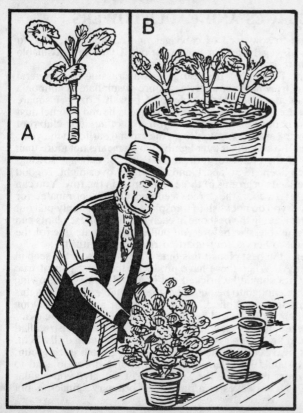

GERANIUM CUTTINGS

It is now time to take cuttings of the ever-popular geraniums that many of us use in our bedding schemes. These, strictly speaking, should be called zonal pelargoniums, but they are still "geraniums" to most people.

Go over your plants and select those shoots that are sturdy, close-jointed and flowerless if possible. If you have to use shoots which have formed buds, remove the buds. Cut each shoot, with a sharp razor-blade, for example, straight across immediately below a leaf joint. Remove the lower leaves. You should then have a cutting 3 or 4 in. long similar in appearance to that shown in inset A.

These cuttings can then be left overnight on a dry shelf (in the shade) to allow a cork-like skin to form over the cut surface. This helps to prevent the stem rotting before it has formed roots after being potted up. If you do this you do not dip the end in hormone rooting powder before insertion in the potting compost.

Other people prefer to omit the drying period and to use hormone rooting powder, potting up the cuttings immediately they have been prepared. You may like to experiment, doing half the cuttings one way and half the other to see which method gives you the best results.

For the compost, you can use John Innes No. 1 or one of the soil-less potting composts. If you wish to prepare your own, use 2 parts of good, fine loam, 2 parts silver sand and 4 parts peat.

The cuttings are inserted for half their length in pots (5 or 6 to a 5 in. pot, for example) round the edge (inset B), or in boxes, sufficiently far apart that their leaves do not touch. Make the cuttings quite firm, pressing the compost round them with the fingers. Moisten the compost, preferably without wetting the leaves, and stand in the shade. At this time of year, I prefer to put them out-of-doors but they can go into the greenhouse if you can give them a shaded place—under the staging, for instance. Do not water again until really necessary, but remember that soil-less compost must never be allowed to get really dry.

CABBAGES AND CAULIFLOWERS

There is still time to sow seed of cabbages and cauliflowers, etc., to ensure a supply of vegetables for use in spring, if you have available some ground where crops have been harvested.

To increase the fertility of the soil give it a dressing of a general fertiliser, such as Growmore, or apply a mixture of sulphate of ammonia 1 oz., superphosphate 2 oz., and sulphate of potash ½ oz. per square yard. Also give a dressing of lime (if your soil needs it) and calomel dust (according to instructions on container) if you are bothered by club root or have been growing similar vegetables on the ground earlier in the year.

Having dressed the soil, dig it over lightly, which means not more than six inches deep. If the area is dry, draw the drills for cabbage sowing, about half an inch deep, 18 in. apart, and water well over-night. A good plan is to sow the seeds in groups of three, 6 in. apart in the row. You can then, later on, lift two of the three seedlings, if all germinate, for transplanting or, if you do not wish to transplant, you can simply pull out the surplus plants, leaving the best one in each position. These plants can be left to get to a usable size before you pull each alternate one for the kitchen leaving the others a foot apart to reach full maturity.

For cauliflowers, the best plan at this time of year is to sow the seed in a seed-box (inset A). When these have produced their first pair of true leaves, the seedlings should be pricked out in a cold-frame for growing on into plants large enough to be put out in the vegetable plot. When this is done, all plants that are "blind", that is, without a central growing point, as shown in inset B, should be discarded as they will be useless.

Two other vegetables to sow now are Spinach Beet (also called Perpetual Spinach) and Winter Radish. Both can be sown in drills 15 in. apart, in groups of 3 seeds, 8 in. apart, removing 2 from each group. Winter Radishes should be lifted in the autumn and stored in sand to keep them for winter use, while the Spinach Beet will give you regular pickings of fresh green leaves at a time when ordinary spinach is not available.

ONIONS AND SHALLOTS

By now shallots should be ready for harvesting, as can be judged by the yellowing of the foliage. If they are, they should be lifted, preferably during a nice sunny spell. Shake off the soil and turn each cluster upside down to dry in the sun. If you can't dry them in this way place them, upside-down, in a greenhouse or garage, or even under cloches in the open. They must be left like this until thoroughly dry, particularly if you want to store them for use during the winter, like onions.

When quite dry, separate each bulb, clean off all earth, loose skin, etc., and set aside the number of medium sized ones that you wish to save for planting next year, making quite sure the wife knows that these are *not* for use in the kitchen! The others (if you aren't using them for pickled "onions") should be stored in boxes in single layers or in nets. *Don't* use plastic bags or they will rot, or even grow!

At this time of year we should also be paying attention to the harvesting of onions. If the foliage has not yet turned yellow and fallen over but the bulbs appear to have reached maturity give nature a helping hand by turning over the tops, bending carefully at the neck, in alternate directions along the rows as shown in inset A. This helps the ripening process by stopping the sap flow. Don't let the foliage lie across another bulb and shade it as the rays of the sun are essential.

When the foliage has obviously died, the onions should be lifted, taking care not to bruise them. They should then be left, upside-down, on the surface to ripen in the sun. If this isn't possible out of doors lay them out similarly under cover, preferably in greenhouse or under cloches where the sun can reach them. They must be thoroughly cleaned, dried and ripened or they will not keep through the winter.

Don't remove the yellowed tops unless you are going to store them in boxes, like apples. It is better to use the tops to tie them in ropes and store them in this way in a cool dry shed or garage. While they are hanging up in this way it is as well to turn them round once a month, to give all the bulbs equal opportunities for light, air, etc.

MAKING A NEW LAWN

The most important factor in the making of a new lawn is the preparation of the soil.

The ground must be thoroughly dug over to a depth of about 9 in., removing as you do so all large stones and roots of perennial weeds.

If you wish to turn a slope into a level area, remove the top soil and carry out the levelling with the sub-soil. Then return the top soil. This ensures that you have an even depth of top soil over the entire site—an essential requirement for even growth all over.

Once the area has been dug and raked level leave it for a few weeks to allow all the annual weed seeds to germinate. These can then be killed off easily with a weed-killer. There are several on the market which will do this without harming the soil or adversely affecting the germination of grass seed, as they act only on plant growth, becoming inactive as soon as they touch the ground. Treading evenly all over the surface, when dry, helps to consolidate the ground.

The surface should then again be levelled. Use a "lute" as in inset A for this. This tool can be bought or easily made by a handyman, the essential point about it being that the head swivels on the handle.

The area should then be marked out in yard squares—which enables you easily to calculate how much seed or how many turves (usually cut 2 or 3 ft. by 1 ft.) you require. Sow seed 2 oz. per square yard, sowing a quarter of it in each direction as shown in inset B. Get seed treated with a bird repellent and choose seed to suit the type of lawn you require, i.e., a luxury one mainly for appearance or one intended for hard wear by playing children, etc. Buy the best seed you can afford, using, say, only 1½ ozs. a yard of good seed rather than 2 oz. of cheap seed.

If you are going to lay turves, start round the edges and work towards the centre. As with seed, buy the best turf you can, as good turf is difficult to obtain. Remember, "weed-treated" means exactly that—it doesn't guarantee it is weed-*free*! Examine carefully before you order. September is *the* lawn-making month, so start now.

WINTER-FLOWERING SHRUBS

It may seem strange that in the middle of August I am already writing about winter. I make no apology for this, as one of the secrets of successful gardening is the ability to look sufficiently far ahead.

Almost without exception our gardens are unnecessarily lacking in colour in the winter. We may have some evergreens (in which there is a good variety of leaf shades) and some colour in the form of berries, such as those of cotoneaster, but what about some actual *flowers*, apart, usually, from winter jasmine?

The important thing is to order in advance and to know what to order, of course. The sites, too, should be prepared now. Dig each hole about 2 ft. deep and at least as much across. Break up sub-soil, to improve drainage, but don't bring it to the surface. Cover it with a good dressing of leaf-mould, peat, well-rotted manure, etc., to enrich it because once your shrub is planted you cannot do any enrichment afterwards, except by surface mulching. Each site will then be nicely settled down by planting time in the autumn.

Now for a few suggested subjects. Inset A shows Garrya elliptica, sometimes called "Tassel Bush" from the grey-green, silky catkins, borne in January/February, which make a striking contrast to the foliage. It is evergreen, is quick-growing and can be used very effectively against a wall.

B shows Hamamelis mollis or Chinese Witch-Hazel. This produces what are probably the most curious winter flowers there are. Against its bare branches, it throws out bunches of twisted petal strips, yellow with red bases, which have been called "fairy fingers". They are scented, seem to be immune to frost and last for weeks. From this shrub we also have a "bonus" in the autumn, when the hazel-like green leaves turn a golden yellow before falling.

C shows Prunus Subhirtella Autumnalis, which is very valuable as another small tree or shrub flowering on bare branches in winter. "Rosea" is the best form, having pale pink flowers of flowering-cherry type.

ROSE CUTTINGS AND LAYERING

Now is the time to increase your stock of roses by cuttings and layering.

The plants you produce in this way may not be quite up to professional standards as far as vigour and robustness are concerned because those you buy are budded on to specially-selected rooting stocks in order to obtain these very qualities. But the new plants will grow into bushes that are quite satisfactory to the average home gardener.

They will, in fact, have one great advantage over bought bushes, in that all growth they produce will produce flowers of that variety. They will never produce any suckers, because they have no common rootstock (from which suckers grow) as their roots are their own.

The shoots to select for cuttings are good firm ones produced this year which haven't flowered. Pull (not cut) them off in a downward direction so that there is a "heel" of old wood attached, about an inch long. Cut off the tip, remove the lower leaves and trim the heel to a neat shape as shown in inset A. The cutting should then be 8-10 in. long.

Take out a narrow trench with a spade so that one side slopes at an angle of about 45°. Put into the bottom 4 or 5 in. of peat and sand (equal parts). Dip the bottom of each cutting into water, then into a hormone rooting powder and push the cuttings into the peat and sand, 6 in. apart, leaving about half their length above ground level. Fill in the trench with nice friable soil and tread firm.

An alternative method is shown in inset B. The cuttings are similarly treated, except that they are then placed in a glass jam-jar of water, supported on a piece of cardboard. When rooted, they must be planted out.

Rambler roses can also be increased now—by layering. A good strong shoot is bent down and a slit made on the underside where it touches the ground. Insert a match or a small piece of wood in the slit to keep it open and peg the stem firmly down to the ground, supporting the remainder of the shoot with a tie or two to a firm stake, as in inset C. Cover the slit, peg, etc., with soil.

STRAWBERRY BARREL

Here is an opportunity to do some gardening for those who do not have a garden. Any patio or similar space that gets a reasonable amount of sunshine will be suitable for growing strawberries in a barrel. Of course, even if you have a garden you may like to try this space-saving method of fruit production.

Having obtained your barrel, which should not be difficult, drill 1 in. holes 4 or 5 in. apart all over the bottom for drainage. After that, screw 3 or 4 castors to the bottom so that you can move the barrel easily, and so turn it round to ensure that all sides have an equal share of sunshine.

If your barrel does not have suitable holes in the sides for the plants, these will have to be cut out next. A key-hole saw is probably the best implement to use for this job. The holes should be about 2½ in. in diameter, and they should be evenly spaced all round the barrel about a foot apart. Avoid making one hole directly under another as far as you can.

A 2 in. layer of broken crocks, bricks, stones, etc., is placed in the bottom to ensure that water can drain out of the holes. Over that place a 2 in. layer of turfy loam or similar moisture-retaining material.

You next need a piece of piping, such as a short length of plastic drainpipe, to place in the centre. As work proceeds, you fill the pipe with pea shingle and surround it with compost (John Innes No. 3 is very suitable). When the compost reaches the first ring of holes, insert the plants in these (from the outside) and continue filling with compost. Repeat as each ring of holes is reached, at the same time partially withdrawing the piping, so as to leave a core of shingle in the compost as a drainage channel from top to bottom.

A barrel usually accommodates about 20 plants, not forgetting that you plant the top of the barrel as well as in the holes at the sides. One barrel should, therefore, provide you with a good quantity of fruit for 3 or 4 years.

The plants should be adequately watered immediately after planting and at all subsequent times must be kept nicely moist.

FREESIAS AND IXIAS

I have yet to meet anyone who isn't enchanted with the deliciously fragrant flowers of freesias in bloom in the early part of the year, say from Jan. to Mar. So why not try a few this year? They need to be planted by the end of Sept. You need a greenhouse, conservatory or room in which you can give them a temperature of 50° to 60°F. later on but they are started in a cold-frame. The corms are usually sold in tens or dozens, which gives you enough for two 5 in. pots.

The best potting mixture consists of good garden soil (preferably some in which there is some well-rotted manure) and sandy loam in equal parts. To this add some sharp sand. Mix it well and fill the two 5 in. pots. In each, place 5 or 6 corms about an inch deep. Each pot is then sunk to its rim in the soil in a cold-frame and the top covered with an inch of light sandy soil. Keep this nicely moist by watering lightly through a rosed can once a day in a really hot spell or 3 times a week in normal dry weather. In about 3 weeks the first growth should appear. This will split into two at first. Later, when there are seven leaves to a corm, the pots should be taken up and placed in full light and air in a greenhouse or similar place in a temperature of 50°F. At this stage they need more water than before to keep them growing steadily.

Only gentle forcing is required and after a fortnight they should be ready to take 60°F. but one must be careful not to overdo the heat or the plants will become spindly and the flowers won't last long.

There are a number of different named varieties available with flower colour ranging from pure white to yellow, pink, orange, blue and similar shades.

We also now have available a novelty in the form of double freesias in several different shades. My own favourite is one called Corona, a deep golden yellow. Corms of these doubles are not usually obtainable until the second half of Sept. so you have plenty of time to order. Freesias are shown in inset A, while B shows Ixias which can be grown in the same way.

TURNIP TOPS

I have no doubt that fresh vegetables are going to be very expensive next winter and in the early part of next year. Therefore, it is very important for every gardener to produce the maximum quantity of crops that will be ready for use during that period.

One way to do this is to re-plant land as it becomes vacant and a crop to sow for this purpose is the turnip. This may surprise some people and may provoke the reaction that "we don't like turnips". I should, therefore, immediately explain that these are not grown as a root crop but for the turnip tops which serve excellently as "spring greens".

When a piece of land that has been manured for a previous crop becomes vacant fork it over lightly and give it a dressing of nitrate of soda, 1 oz. to the square yard, or bone-meal, 5 oz. to the square yard. Rake it in and tread the ground reasonably firm. Sow the seed ½ in. deep in drills 1 ft. apart. Water the drills thoroughly before sowing the seed if the weather is dry.

Most seedsmen stock a variety especially suitable for this purpose, usually called Green Globe, Green Round, or Green Top. The plants will stand the winter and if sown thinly may not need thinning. If when they germinate they are obviously too thick, thin to about 6 in. apart as shown in inset A. If they need watering to get them well-established, do it in the evening. A dusting of derris will keep them free of pests.

Those who are already growing turnips can produce a second crop for themselves by cutting off the crowns of the roots when they are used and planting them in a seed-box, as shown in inset B. Use potting compost in the box and place it in a warm dark place, in a shed or under the greenhouse staging. Keep the compost nicely moist and soon you will see long, blanched stalks on which are the small white leaves for cooking. As a gourmet's vegetable they take some beating and if you have never tried them you are in for a very pleasant surprise, which also applies to the tops grown out-of-doors as they have a flavour all their own.

TULIPS—THE MIRACLE OF THE BULB

THE TULIP, a member of the lily family, is indeed a remarkable plant. There are tulips in all colours of the rainbow from the purplish black of Queen of the Night to the palest pink of Princess Margaret, from the yellow of Tarakan to the violet of The Bishop.

There are blooms that are slim and graceful, and others that have waved, crested and frilly petals. There are flowers which are shaded, streaked and tinged. The viridiflora tulips even have a touch of green in their blooms. There are tulips which soar to 28in. and others which remain a petite 4in.

Nowadays there are 15 distinctly different groups of tulips, offering a choice of hundreds of different bulbs. In fact there is no other plant on earth which offers the gardener such an immense choice of colours and combination of colours. It was in fact the brilliance of the colours that gave tulips their initial popularity.

Rather like the child who stands at the sweetshop counter, bewildered by the choice of goodies, it is no easy matter making up one's mind which of all the many beautiful tulips to grow.

So let me help you. And surely the logical place to start is at the beginning of the year.

For instance, did you know that it is possible to get a tulip to flower *outdoors* in February? You can. It is called Violet Queen and its long-lasting globe-shaped rosy violet flowers are carried on 6in. stems.

In March in my garden, I always look forward to the flaming scarlet flowers of the tulip called Fusilier. Often there are as many as four flowers on *each* 6in. stem, and what a wonderful splash of colour they make.

Also in March there are the small-growing waterlily tulips, all somewhere between 4in. and 10in. high. I like Heart's Delight, which is carmine red with rosy white, and Alfred Cortot, a brilliant red.

April is, at least in the South of England, the real beginning of Tulip Time.

In parts of the North, your tulips may flower as much as two to three weeks later than mine.

In April I look forward to seeing the Greigii tulips with their elegant heads on short stems among the *colourful* leaves. There is Corsage, for example, with apricot blooms and green leaves marked with broken lines of chocolate brown.

For tubs and urns, deep window boxes, and the open garden I strongly recommend the Fosteriana tulip Madame Lefeber. It originated on the mountain slopes of Bokhara and is appropriately enough a rich oriental scarlet. At around 15in. tall, you will be hard pressed to find a more beautiful, diminutive tulip for your garden.

April, too, sees the appearance of the 15in. high single tulip, such as the lovely sun gold Bellona and the crimson Cassini, which is another tulip well-suited to growing in tubs.

Most tulips are not noted for their perfume, but De Wet, which is a glorious golden orange, is the exception with a heady sweet scent.

For northern gardens, or places cruelly exposed to easterly winds, the brilliant crimson and yellow flowers of Keizerskroon can take the worst our climate has to offer.

If the weather is your worry, then you should select tulips which are not particularly tall. For example, the 11in. high rosy pink double tulip called Peach Blossom. It is very effective planted in groups of five or ten in a shrub border or among other plants.

Next we come to two very important groups of tulips —the Darwin hybrids and the famous Darwins themselves.

Darwin *hybrids* have been bred from the Darwin parents to produce larger flowers on stronger stems. In late April they are magnificent. General Eisenhower is the name of the tulip with probably the largest flowers of all tulips. The petals are the red of a Guardsman's tunic and they have a sheen of which any soldier would be proud.

The Darwins flower in May. The 27in. tall Heather Hill, which is a delightful heather pink, perfectly illustrates the traditional Darwin shape, conical closed and like a tumbler when open. The pink Queen Bartigon is an excellent Darwin tulip for windy gardens even although it is 25in. tall.

In May I like to see too the raspberry red on white of the 25in. tall Rembrandt tulip called Union Jack and the fluted flowers of Apricot Parrot.

Some people like tulips to cut and to take indoors. For this purpose you cannot do better than the lily flowering tulips China Pink and Inimitable, which is a buttercup yellow. That is, if you can bear to cut them; for these distinctly elegant tulips are a delight when planted in groups in the border.

In a similar position the viridiflora tulip Pimpernell, with its turkey red petals, each with a green blaze, looks quite at home among the fresh green growth of the border plants which will flower everywhere in June.

And finally what about some cottage tulips? The modern kinds are strong and sturdy. Try growing one like the long-lasting Mirella with its buff, rose-shaped petals, each with a blaze of raspberry red rising from the base.

Once you have made your selection, you should order the bulbs immediately to ensure that you can get the ones you want, although there is actually no need to plant them before the middle of November.

Earlier planting may simply encourage the bulbs to grow too fast and expose tender new growth to frost. This even applies to tulips which will flower in February and March.

Tulips, which are extremely hardy plants, will grow in any soil that is not waterlogged. The bulbs should be planted 6in. apart and covered with 6in. of soil, except in light sandy soil where the bulbs should be 12in. deep.

Tulips, unfortunately, can fall victim to certain diseases. The worst of these is Tulip Fire which is death to tulips. So before you put the bulbs in the ground take the precaution of dipping them for 15 minutes in a solution of benomyl fungicide.

Also when planting add a few slug pellets to the soil to get rid of these nibbling pests.

BULBS IN BOWLS

Nothing helps to brighten the long, dark days of winter more than some nice bowls of bulbs in flower over the Christmas period or early in the new year. By starting them at different times or by using different subjects or varieties, quite a long flowering succession can be achieved.

Most people are now familiar with the fibre-in-bowls method so why not try other ways this year? Some bulbs can be grown for early flowering in this way entirely on water, which not only saves the cost of the fibre but also provides a novelty.

The bulbs to use are crocus, the narcissus varieties Bridal Crown, Cragford and Paper White, or the white Roman hyacinths.

One way is to use a wide, shallow bowl in the bottom of which is placed an inch or so of sand or shingle. On this, pebbles are spaced out so that the bulbs can be arranged among them, not too close together, in such a way that the pebbles hold the bulbs as firmly in position as possible and at the same time keep the base of each bulb just above the level of the sand. It is important that the bulbs do not "sit" in water as they then tend to rot.

It is a great advantage to use rain-water, even when adding more later. (Even in a flat you can put an empty bowl out on a window- sill to catch rain for this purpose.)

Keep the bowl of bulbs in a cool, dark place until growth has started. You can then bring it into the light, but not immediately into direct sunlight. Keep the water at the correct level at all times.

Another method is shown in the inset in what is often called a hyacinth-glass. Again, use rain-water and place a few lumps of charcoal in the bottom. Keep in darkness until you can see that roots have formed, then bring into the light. You can then watch its progress, which is quite fascinating. Don't try to force it too quickly with too much heat or the leaves will be much taller than the flowers.

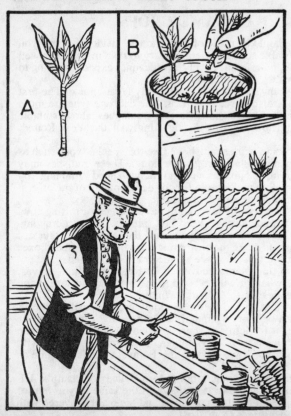

TAKING CUTTINGS

Apart from the actual production of food crops, it should not be forgotten that we can make considerable savings by raising our own plants by rooting cuttings of those we already have. A remarkable number of different plants can be increased in this way at this time of year. For example, Penstemon, Calceolaria, Viola, Pansy, Petunia, Verbena, Marguerite and Fuchsia, to mention but a few. There are many more—and why not experiment to see if you can succeed in surprising your friends, perhaps?

Cuttings taken now should have time to root and develop into quite sturdy little plants that will survive the winter. It is best to use shoots which have not flowered, of the present season's growth. Prepare them so that they look like the one shown in inset A, cutting neatly across the stem, immediately below a leaf joint and removing the lower leaves. Wet the end, dip it in hormone rooting powder and insert in holes made with a pencil or something similar in pots, boxes (deeper than normal seed-boxes) or direct in a cold-frame as shown in insets B and C.

A good mixture for them is one part each of good loam, peat and silver sand or one of the soilless cutting composts. It should be nicely moist when you insert the cuttings, watering it overnight and allowing it to drain before insertion, if necessary. Afterwards, it should be kept just nicely moist, carefully avoiding over-watering. The cuttings need a sheltered spot not in full sunlight. This is usually not difficult to arrange with easily movable pots or boxes. Where the cold-frame is concerned, cover it with some sacking, or something similar, to keep off excessive sunlight but don't destroy the ventilation in the process, otherwise the cuttings may damp off before rooting.

By using hormone rooting powder the rooting process is speeded up. Most of these cuttings will be rooted in about 3 weeks. I have had fuchsia cuttings treated in this way rooted in two weeks.

When they have rooted, as evidenced by new growths, keep them outside as long as possible so that they develop into sturdy, hardy plants, only taking inside when frost arrives.

COLD-FRAME CROPS

More intensive use should be made of cold frames. Inside the frame you need good fertile, friable soil, sufficiently peaty to hold moisture as well as sufficiently sandy to drain effectively. You cannot expect anything to grow well in the winter in cold wet clay.

What should we grow? There is a surprisingly large choice. The first that springs to mind, of course, is lettuce. The cabbage type are more likely to be successful than the cos. All catalogues show suitable varieties for sowing now such as Arctic King, All the Year Round, Unrivalled, etc.

Then how about some winter radishes? Use the special types such as China Rose or Spanish Black, round or long. These radishes may produce roots weighing as much as a pound each, so need "thinning" by using some when small to make room for the development of the others. They are used shredded or sliced in salads.

Mustard and cress is a crop you may not have thought of raising now. Stretch a piece of flannel across a seed-box, and fasten with drawing-pins, as in inset A. Moisten the flannel and sow the seed on top, mustard 4 days after the cress, to make the crop coincide in maturing. Such boxes can be kept in the kitchen, if space in the frame is needed.

Another idea is to transplant one root of herbs such as mint, chives, etc., into the frame where it will respond to the better environment and give you fresh supplies all through the winter.

Endive is a plant that should be more widely grown, particularly for winter salads. It can be treated similarly to lettuce and can, in fact, be used as a replacement for lettuce. There are two main types, the green curled and the lettuce-leaved or Batavian. Both need covering with flower-pots to blanch the leaves, while the Batavian needs tying up as well, as shown in inset B.

Inset C shows another suggestion—corn salad or lamb's lettuce—which you may not know. It is grown in the same way as lettuce but the leaves are picked singly as required and the plants covered with straw or bracken to protect from frost.

SEPTEMBER   First Week

USE OF CLOCHES

One of the best ways to prolong the productivity of our gardens as we move into the autumn is by the use of cloches. At this season many people tend to put them away for use again next year but they can still stimulate growth so that one can have extra or later crops for use in the winter.

Placed over a row of young lettuce, for example, the cloches will still make considerable improvement in the timing and size of the resultant crop. Use the tent type (inset A) over low-growing plants such as cabbage lettuce and the barn-type (inset B) over taller ones such as cos lettuce.

Provided the soil is nicely moist, as it probably will be at this time of year, when you put the cloches on, you can keep it that way without removing the cloches by simply watering, if that is necessary, over the glass. It will run through the spaces and under the lower edges of the glass and spread on to the soil inside the glass quite effectively.

One important thing to remember is that the glass of the cloches should be really clean as we need it to allow in as much light as possible, now that the days are drawing in and we aren't getting any too much sunshine anyway.

Inset C shows a useful little gadget. It is simply a wooden block with two grooves sawn in it at suitable angles so that it will hold in place two separate sheets of glass to make a tent type cloche. Most people have a number of pieces of glass that can be used in this way—often the remaining portions where one side of a cloche has broken.

Even if you haven't any young lettuce plants to cover, you can still sow seed, choosing a variety that will stand the winter. Every catalogue has at least one. And how about sowing some Early Nantes carrots so that you have nice fresh young carrots to pull for Christmas dinner?

Cloches can also be used advantageously now to cover a patch of parsley, mint, etc., of which a supply of fresh green leaves comes in very handy in winter-time.

BULBS FOR SHADY SPOTS

Several kinds of bulbs for shady spots can be planted during the next few weeks. Scatter handfuls of the bulbs, planting them where they fall.

Use a trowel if the site is of soil. Drop a little sand and bone-meal into each hole; set the bulb at its correct depth and refill the hole. If the site is rough turf, use a strong dibber, packing fine soil round the bulb.

Winter Aconites massed among trees and shrubs make a colourful sight. Spring-flowering bulbs to occupy spaces under trees are Bluebells and Scillas. Sandy loam suits them, but they grow quite well in ordinary garden soil. Set the small kinds 2 in. to 3 in. deep; the larger ones 5 in. to 6 in.

Other shade-loving bulbs to be planted not later than the end of September are Chionodoxa, 2 in. to 3 in. deep, and Snowdrops. Meadow Saffron (Colchicum) massed under leaf-losing trees or in shade among grass provide a good show. Set their tops 2 in. below soil level. Plant Daffodils in a grass corner which can be left uncut for as long as possible. Lift turf, plant bulbs and replace grass.

Unlike Persian Cyclamen, so popular as a pot plant in flower around Christmas time, the miniature, hardy Cyclamen, which deserves equal popularity, is comparatively little known. It likes limy soil and leaf-mould in a shady position. Plant 2 in. deep, 6 in. apart now or next month. Some of these Cyclamen root from the top of the corm so make sure there is 2 in. of soil above each corm. These are good for a dry spot.

They succeed in places where scarcely anything else will grow, between the major roots of trees close to the trunk for instance where you have very little depth of soil. In such situations give them every year a top dressing of leaf-mould but otherwise leave them alone. They will reward you wonderfully with a charming display of their tiny flowers in ever-widening circles as the years go by. As a general rule one doesn't use manure with bulbs but I have gained remarkably improved results with these Cyclamen—often called coum hybrids, by the way—by mixing well-rotted cow-manure half and half with the leaf-mould for their top dressing.

A   B

LAYERING BERRY FRUITS

One good way of increasing home fruit production is to raise new plants of such fruits as loganberries and cultivated blackberries. If you have at least one bush of each of these fruits, now is the time to do what is called layering, which is merely the rooting of new growths. This is well worth while with these particular fruits because the quantity of crop per foot of cane, as it were, is probably higher than in any other kind.

Layering can be done in two ways—tip layering or serpentine layering. Which method you adopt depends on how many suitable long shoots you have on your plants and on how many new plants you wish to produce.

Inset A shows tip layering, in which the end of the shoot is pegged down into the soil and covered, as shown.

The other method, shown in inset B, is really the same thing except that the cane is pegged down at intervals of about 18 in. along its length. In this case, do not peg down the tip as well as this will draw all the nourishment from the other pegged down points and few of them usually root.

If your soil is not sufficiently light and friable for the plant to make roots in it easily, the best plan is to sink pots in the soil at the appropriate places and to fill these pots with a mixture of equal parts of light soil, peat and sand. Then peg the canes down in these pots.

In the spring, the cane is severed close to the peg and the new plants dug up and replanted where required.

Any remaining pieces of cane sufficiently long can then be tied up to the fence or other support for fruiting in the normal way later on.

If you can then give all the plants, old and new alike, a nice mulch of manure they will respond to it with much more vigorous growth.

For anyone planning to grow such fruit, I recommend a *thornless* variety of blackberry. It makes fruit-picking so much more pleasant—even the ladies will do it! Plant them this autumn.

AMARYLLIS

So many more people nowadays are growing Amaryllis (more correctly called Hippeastrum) that a number of readers request advice on their cultivation. These bulbs are really quite easy, particularly for those who have no way of providing the necessary warmth other than their central heating indoors. But more of that later.

The first requirement, apart from ordering the bulbs (which should be in bloom by Christmas if planted immediately on arrival in early October) is to prepare the correct soil mixture. This should consist of equal parts of good medium loam and leaf-mould, plus a generous helping of coarse, silver sand, so that the whole mixture drains very well and never remains too wet. Pots should be used that are only about 1 in. larger in circumference than the bulb itself.

They should be scrubbed clean in disinfectant water. Ample crocks must be placed in the bottom unless you are using plastic pots which already have adequate drainage holes. In the bottom of the pot place a mound of the compost so that the roots can be draped over it as shown in inset A. But before planting, the roots and lower half of the bulb should be soaked in lukewarm water, renewing it as necessary, for four or five days. When the bulb has been planted add more compost to bring the top of it level about 1 in. down from the pot rim, leaving the upper half of the bulb exposed.

Sufficient tepid water should be given to keep the compost just moist for the first fortnight or until growth commences. Once this happens, a little more water should be given as necessary but always use warm water and never allow the pot to stand in water that has drained through.

Ideally, the pot from the beginning should be given bottom heat. This is easy enough in greenhouse or propagating frame for the expert but is also easy for the amateur in the home, who can stand the pot on the mantelpiece above the fireplace or on a window-sill above a radiator. Once buds have formed it should be placed in a sunny position, such as a window-sill, to complete the flowering period.

SWEET-PEAS

Those of us who wish to produce fine stems of sweet-pea blooms as early as possible next year should start the preparations now. This means taking out the top spit from a trench and digging into the second spit a generous helping of manure or some substitute for it (such as hop manure) which can be easily obtained. The seed is sown at the end of the month or early October.

Before sowing, it is as well to soak the seeds in water for 24 hours to make the seeds swell and to make the skins easier to break. This applies particularly to the black-skinned varieties. It is not so important with the others. Any seeds which have failed to swell should have the skin chipped with a small knife, on the side opposite the "eye", to ensure as even germination as possible. Those seeds which have swollen should germinate satisfactorily without chipping.

When your trench has been properly prepared, the top soil having been returned, of course, and it has had the benefit, I hope, of some rain and weathering, draw a drill in it two or three inches deep. Sow the seed in this as the higher sides will give some weather protection later and will also enable you to draw some soil up to the plants in due course when they are growing strongly.

Sowing in this way is particularly suitable for those people who have light soil or soil that is well-drained. If you can give them cloche protection during the severest weather so much the better but they should stand the winter without it.

For those whose soil is considered unsuitable for this treatment the seed can be sown in pots (of John Innes compost for preference) and the pots kept in a cold frame for the winter. They should be grown "hard", they do not need any protection except from snow or exceptionally heavy rain. Too much water is fatal. For that reason when sowing the seed in pots, don't water for two days, then soak them and keep nicely moist all through the germination period.

If you cannot adopt either of these methods you will have to wait until Jan. or Feb. to sow in a greenhouse, or Mar. or Apr. out-of-doors.

TOMATO RIPENING

We are now entering the season when the many people who are growing tomatoes out-of-doors are beginning to wonder just how much of their crop they are going to get ripe. Even if it has been a good season for them that is no reason why we should not do all we can to obtain the maximum benefit from our labours. Green tomatoes can, of course, be used for chutney very profitably but ripe fruit are so much more acceptable and useful.

The basic requirement is an adequate supply of moisture in the soil the roots are growing in—which doesn't mean merely the surface of the ground. Rain-water is to be preferred—direct from the heavens, we hope—but, if not, man-handled from a water butt. One reason for this is that the temperature of water stored in a butt is that much higher than that from the tap.

The next thing is adequate potash. Even if you have been feeding your plants with a tomato fertiliser, as I hope you have, some additional potash may be required to speed up the ripening process. It must be realised that ripening is not merely a matter of the fruit hanging in the sunshine until it becomes "sunburnt", as it were, it is a growth or development process which will continue after the fruit is picked—even in the darkness of a drawer, as shown in inset B.

Give each plant a teaspoonful of potash once a week and water it in.

Other methods can be used, such as pinning plastic over them if they are against a fence, as shown in the main drawing, or the plants can be removed from their supports and carefully laid on a thick layer of straw, with cloches placed over them (inset A) to give them additional warmth.

It is important to adopt measures of this kind to get as many fruits ripe on the plants before picking them, as artificial ripening does not produce as good a flavour as the natural way.

On the other hand, it does help the green ones to ripen if you pick those which have changed colour fairly early and let them finish the process indoors. It is really a matter of using one's discretion according to the amount of fruit on the plants that has not yet matured.

VEGETABLE SOWINGS

With the prospect of vegetables further increasing in price, particularly during the winter and early spring when they are never very plentiful, it is essential that we all try to obtain the maximum amount of produce from our gardens.

For this reason, land that becomes vacant as crops are harvested should immediately be re-worked ready for the sowing of further vegetables. Assuming it was manured or fertilised for the previous crop, it should not need enriching again, unless it is particularly light soil. Deep digging should also not be necessary unless it has been trodden down into a solid mass in which you obviously cannot sow seed. Dig if you must, but otherwise just loosen the top few inches with the hoe and break it down into a fine tilth ready for drawing shallow seed drills.

Although general fertilisation is not necessary, as we do not want to promote a lot of soft growth that will not stand up to the rigours of the winter, a dressing of bone-meal (2 oz. per square yard) will be beneficial as this is a slow-acting product that will not take effect until early spring.

If the ground is dry, draw the drills overnight and soak them with water, sowing the seed next day when the drill has nicely drained.

Lettuces are one vegetable to treat in this way. One of the largest and best varieties for autumn sowing is Imperial Winter, shown in inset A, but this variety is not for sowing at other times of the year. To avoid buying too many packets of seed, you could use a variety called Unrivalled which is one of the best for winter or summer. The seed is sown ½ in. deep in rows 1 ft. apart and the seedlings thinned to 9 in. apart. If you can put cloches over one row, or part of a row, so that they do not all mature at once, so much the better. Carefully lifted seedlings can be transplanted if you wish.

Another vegetable to sow now is the turnip. Choose one called Golden Ball, shown in inset B, as it is hardy enough to stand the winter and is usable over a long period. Sowing distances are about the same as for lettuces.

COLD GREENHOUSE BULBS

Those people who have a cold greenhouse—that is, one in which there is no artificial heat in the winter-time—tend to regard it at that time of year mainly as a store shed.

I prefer a much more positive attitude, taking definite steps to grow in it suitable subjects that will flower there that much earlier because they have had some protection.

How pleasing it is on a dull, wintry day to find in a greenhouse some flowers bravely coming into bloom. No doubt you all know we can use certain bulbs in this way, so let's see what else we can use.

Provided you use John Innes or a soil-less compost—or its equivalent made up by yourself—there should be no growing problem.

The insets show three suitable suggestions. A is Erythronium, often called Dog's Tooth Violet. This not only produces long-petalled flowers ranging from white to pink, lilac and purple but also has marbled leaves which give one an attractive foliage plant, even without the flowers.

B is Iris histrioides, of which there are several named varieties, mainly blue. Then there's I. reticulata with even more named varieties, purple as well as blue. And one should not forget I. unguicularis, known to many as stylosa, whose charming flowers do not last long when cut unfortunately. All these should be in bloom between the end of Dec. and Feb.

Our third inset shows Fritillaria meleagris or Snake's Head Fritillary. It gets its name from its habit of hanging its head as shown in snake fashion. The flower colouring ranges from white to light grey and dark purple, some having a most attractive mottled appearance. My own favourite is one called Purple King, a dark winy purple.

Quite a number of plants normally grown outside can be speeded up in flowering in this way. Try a few Wallflowers, Auriculas, Polyanthus, winter flowering Pansies, Solomon's Seal, etc.

Ventilate the house whenever the weather is suitable and try to keep the internal atmosphere as dry as possible. If you must do any watering, do it first thing in the morning.

GOOSEBERRIES—SO EASY TO GROW

GOOSEBERRIES are great for the garden. They are so easy to grow and the fruit has so many uses.

Easy, because they prefer a cool temperate climate like ours. This is one fruit for which you will not be able to blame the weather for lack of success. Cool growing conditions actually lead to better crops.

Gooseberries can be made into jam or jelly, pies and flans, fools and soufflés. They are also excellent for freezing, which means that this summer fruit can be "in season," so far as your lunch menus are concerned, all year round.

The prickly bushes produce their crops from the second half of May to August, depending on the variety you choose and where you live. For convenience, I shall refer to them as early (May fruiting), mid season (June) and late (July) to give you some idea when you can expect the fruit.

Gooseberries can either be grown as solitary bushes, which incidentally will thrive in full sun or shade, or you can have special types of bushes called "cordons" which can be trained against wires on walls and fences.

Let me explain: a cordon is a gooseberry with just one main branch and lots of little fruit-producing side shoots. The beauty of it, especially if you are short of space, is that you can have a row of gooseberries 18 in. apart; whereas with the normal bush, you would have to allow 5 ft. between each one. The fruit is also easier to pick from a cordon because there are fewer prickles.

Cordons can be grown on north-facing walls and fences, which is a position that does not find favour with many other plants and shrubs.

With the ordinary bushes, there is no need to give them a special place to themselves. Gooseberries are perfectly happy and quite attractive with their tiny, pale green lobed leaves among other shrubs and plants.

For that gooseberry pie you could choose a variety like Keepsake. It produces the earliest of all firm green berries for picking for pies. Then later it develops plump, soft sweet berries for dessert.

This is the key to getting the best results from each bush. Top quality berries are produced by thinning the fruit early and using the small green berries (the "thinnings") as the fillings for pies and tarts.

As well as the early variety Keepsake, you can choose from Whitesmith, New Giant and Early Sulphur to obtain the first gooseberries of the season.

If you live in an area where blossom and fruit destroying late frosts are common, then I would advise you to concentrate on the following mid-season varieties.

You can have the splendid gooseberry called Careless. It yields large, fine flavoured, slightly furry, almost white berries which are suitable for everything from jam to dessert.

There are also the two red gooseberries Lancashire Lad

and Whinham's Industry and the two yellow gooseberries Leveller and Golden Drop. These are all well-tried varieties, and your local nurseryman will guide you as to the ones which do best in your district.

Even if your garden has the worst possible position, weather-wise, I would be very disappointed indeed if you did not succeed in getting fruit from the late season gooseberries Lancer (yellowish-green berries) and White Lion.

The ideal time to plant is between November and March.

Gooseberries will grow in any ordinary soil, provided it is neither excessively wet in winter nor too dry in summer. I suggest that you fork over the planting position 1 ft. deep and work in some dry peat to make the soil less sticky. No fertilisers are required at this stage.

Let's deal with the ordinary bushes first. They should be planted 5 ft. apart and the soil firmed around their stems with your foot.

The first year after planting you will not have to do any pruning as this will have been done for you by the nursery which supplied the bushes.

In succeeding winters the drill is to cut back the main branches by half to an outward facing bud. The smaller side branches should be trimmed back to the third bud.

Aim to keep the inside of the bush as open as possible and do not worry about being a bit ruthless. The harder you prune (*except* Whinham's Industry) the better and more fruitful the bushes will be.

Now let's consider those space-saving cordons. As I told you earlier, cordons have been trained to form a long, single stem with very short side branches. Such cordons can be grown upright (with support) to 4 ft. to 6 ft. or inclined at an angle to the ground.

You can plant them 18 in. to 2 ft. apart in as many varieties as you wish against any wall or fence. Horizontal wires, secured at 9 in. intervals up to a height of 5 ft., are necessary for support.

You can also train a row of cordons against wires stretched between posts in a position which is in the shade of other fruit trees such as apples. Whinham's Industry is a particularly good variety for these conditions. A second row of cordons should be 5 ft. from the first.

Pruning cordons is easy. You simply take the top six inches off each cordon in February and cut back the side shoots to two or three buds.

I should explain that gooseberries are self-fertile. So even if you have room for just one bush, you will still get fruit.

Apart from pruning, gooseberries do require a little care to ensure that they give the best possible crops.

A thick moisture-retaining (and weed-suppressing) mulch of well-rotted manure, compost or peat in April will help to prevent the soil from drying out. In January give each bush some sulphate of potash at the rate of 1 oz. to a square yard of soil. In March apply sulphate of ammonia at the rate of ½ oz. to 1 oz. to the square yard. The main pests which you may have to deal with are the larvae of the gooseberry sawflies. The remedy is to spray with malathion, soon after the first tiny fruitlets appear. If you are troubled by bullfinches eating the fruit buds in winter, the solution is to cover the bushes with light-weight plastic netting.

CULTIVATED BLACKBERRIES

The name *cultivated* blackberries has always seemed to me to be very apt as they respond extremely well when cultivated properly. Now that fruiting has finished all the old wood should be cut out and the new shoots tied into position, fanning them out against a fence for preference. They then not only have the necessary support but will also benefit from the reflected warmth from the fence.

Stock can be increased now, if required, by the methods shown in the insets. "A" shows how a new shoot can be layered by pegging it down into the ground, or, if your soil is on the heavy side, how the tip of a shoot can be induced to form roots in a pot of sand, soil and peat in equal parts (B). Next spring these can be severed from the parent plant and re-planted where required. Cut them off about 6 in. above soil level, and tie the remainder of the cane back into position.

These blackberries usually produce suckers quite plentifully, some quite often a good way from the parent root. These suckers can be dug up now and replanted to increase your stock.

If you do not have any of these blackberries, now is the time to plant them. I would recommend you choose the thornless ones as this makes pruning, fruit-picking, etc., so much easier.

Although they are not fussy about soil, they prefer deeply cultivated, moist, enriched soil. They should be planted 12 ft. apart, and cut down to 9 in. after planting, to induce them to make new growth.

For both new and old plants, a good top-dressing of potash and sterilised bone-meal is of great benefit, particularly if it is followed, about a month later, by a generous mulch of well-rotted manure or compost about 3 in. deep over an area about a yard in diameter around the base of the plant.

It is important to keep the plants free from perennial weeds but at the same time deep cultivation must be avoided around established plants because they are shallow rooting and tend to spread their roots sideways, not far below the surface, over quite a distance.

SEED SAVING

As a general rule, in normal times, the saving of one's own seed is not to be recommended. Of course, there are exceptions to this rule even when seed can be easily obtained, but at the present time it is much more important to save certain seeds as we are warned of supplies being short and, of course, seed is much more costly. (But it should be borne in mind that the outlay represents a very good investment in relation to the value of the produce obtained.)

Because the seed is usually more expensive, people are being tempted to save seed from F1 hybrid varieties of flowers and vegetables. This is not wise. The resultant plants are unlikely to be true to type, due to cross-pollination. It is this problem of cross-pollination that makes the saving of many other seeds not worthwhile. This applies particularly to the brassica (cabbage) family.

Seeds can be usefully saved from vegetables such as beans, peas, onions, leeks, ridge cucumbers, marrows, lettuces and tomatoes. Good specimens should always be chosen and allowed to ripen naturally as far as possible.

Where you need to separate seeds from chaff, etc., place it in a bowl of water, as shown in inset A. The good seed will sink to the bottom and the rest can be discarded. Dry the seed thoroughly before storing. Inset B shows how to test bean seed. Press each one with the thumb-nail. The skin should dent but not crack.

Seed heads such as those of onions and leeks should be cut with about a foot of stem and the head placed in a paper bag, tied round the stem, and kept so that the seed falls into the bag as it dries and is not lost.

For tomatoes, choose good specimens fully ripe. Cut in half and squeeze pulp and seeds into a bowl. Leave for a couple of days and then wash the pulp off the seeds. Put through a sieve, so as to separate seeds from pulp, and then spread seeds out to dry. When they are thoroughly dry keep in a paper bag. The sooner they are sown the better really although tomato seed retains its vitality for a long time—several years, in fact, although I would not recommend relying on old seed.

FRUIT TREE PLANTING

If you are contemplating putting a few fruit trees in your garden now is the time to get down to it. And by getting down to it I mean the preparation of the soil.

Each site should be dug two spits deep and be a circle or square at least 3 ft. across. Remove the top soil and put it on one side for the moment. Fork over the second spit and spread a good layer of rotted manure or compost over it, before returning the top spit. This manure must be covered with sufficient earth so that the roots do not come into direct contact with it when the trees are planted. The ground should then be left for two or three weeks to settle, before planting.

The next important step is to select and obtain the trees. For this, a visit to a specialist fruit grower is best so that you can discuss with him your exact requirements. The space available is a very important consideration. In a small garden the cordon type, shown in inset A, is probably best because it takes least room. Next to that is the bush type. These types make pruning, spraying and picking much easier than the larger growing forms.

Apart from the type, varieties must be carefully chosen to ensure that pollination will be properly effected. Most people think Cox's Orange Pippin the best eating apple but it needs a pollinator. James Grieve is often used with Cox as each will pollinate the other. Probably the best cooker, Bramley Seedling, needs two pollinators. The Cox can be one but James Grieve will not do as the other. Moreover, Bramley is too vigorous a grower to use as a cordon. From what I have said, you will see that you need to choose very carefully under expert guidance.

The same applies to pears. William and Conference pears (two of the most popular) will pollinate each other, although Conference is self-fertile to some extent. Doyenne du Comice, the best pear, needs Beurre Hardy as pollinator.

Finally, when you have planted your trees give a good mulch of manure or compost, as shown in inset B, to ensure that the roots do not dry out before the trees are established.

OCTOBER Second Week

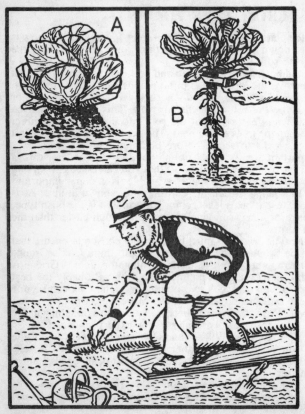

BRUSSELS SPROUTS

All of us should be constantly paying attention to the question of supplying greenstuff for use in the kitchen during the winter. Cabbages, for example, will benefit greatly if earthed up to the lowest leaves, as shown in inset A.

Brussels Sprouts should be supported by stakes to keep them upright. Even when you have finished picking all your sprouts don't pull the plants up. Leave them to develop new head growth and then cut off the tops, as in inset B, as they make an excellent vegetable, when they are of adequate size.

As well as thinking about this year's supply we should also be preparing for the next lot. Brussels Sprouts like a long season of growth and could well be sown now where the ground is in the right condition to make a fine seed-bed, as autumn-sown ones usually produce the best plants. You need a spot sheltered from north and east winds, if possible, where you have not grown any members of the cabbage family for at least a couple of years—perhaps over an area you have removed potatoes from as this will not need further digging.

Unless your land is alkaline enough already, give it a dressing of 4 oz. of hydrated lime plus 1 oz. of superphosphate of lime per sq. yd. Rake this into the surface, tread the ground firm and rake again at right angles to the first raking. Use a board as shown to make shallow drills and to sow the seed. The drills need only be 6 in. apart if you are sowing more than one. Little attention is needed apart from hoeing down the weeds.

These plants you will be able to put into their maturing positions in early spring. They will give a much earlier crop than those sown in spring. March is the time to sow again for a later crop for use after the following Christmas probably. In this way you get a long succession of sprout-picking, which is very welcome in most households. I have never heard anyone complain that they have too many sprouts, either as a gardener or as a consumer!

In order to decide which variety to sow in the autumn seek the advice of a local grower or nurseryman.

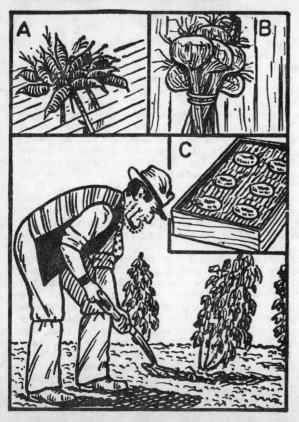

STORING TUBERS

The price of tubers and corms of such worth-while flowers as dahlias, gladioli and begonias being what it is today it is very important to take special care to store them successfully through the winter so that we do not have to buy fresh ones next year.

Dahlias can be safely left in the ground until the early frosts have blackened the foliage. At this stage the tubers will not have been harmed.

Lift the plants carefully, inserting the fork well away from the plant so that you don't spear any of the tubers. Cut the foliage down to about 6 in. of the soil. Clean the soil off the tubers and place them upside-down on the greenhouse staging as shown in inset A. Leave them for a week or two for the tubers to dry and the stalks to drain. They should then be stored in boxes, right way up, and covered with fine, dry soil or sand, leaving the tops of the stems exposed.

Gladioli should be similarly lifted (when the foliage has turned brown) with care, tied in bundles and hung up in a dry shed (see inset B). Leave them there for about a month to let the foliage wither. This is then removed, together with all loose skin, etc., on the corms. These can then be placed in paper bags and stored in a dry, frost-free place. They do not need warmth.

Special care is necessary when lifting begonias to avoid the main stems breaking off the corms. The stems are very brittle and usually rather top heavy. The corms benefit if the foliage remains attached until it has dried off. For this reason the complete plants should be carefully placed in boxes until the foliage has withered. This is then removed and the corms cleaned. Place the corms in boxes of leaf-mould or dry sand, growth side upwards, as shown in inset C. Scoop out a slight hollow for each corm and leave the top surface uncovered. Store in a cool (45 to 50°F.) place that is not too dry as they need a little moisture to prevent them shrivelling.

On the other hand, they must not be sufficiently wet that they rot. To safeguard against this, sprinkle some powdered charcoal over the top to absorb surplus moisture if your store tends to be damp during the winter.

PRUNING SOFT FRUIT

Now is the time of year to prune soft fruit such as gooseberries and the currants, red, white and black. Before one starts, however, it is important to appreciate that the same method is not used for all these fruits, so that one doesn't cut away those parts that are required for fruit production next year. The methods vary because the fruit production habit of all the bushes is not the same.

So let us start with red and white currants whose fruit-bearing habits are the same. The bush consists of leaders, which are the main shoots growing in a generally upward direction, and laterals, which are shoots growing sideways from the leaders. The leaders are shortened to about 6 in. of the current season's growth. The laterals are shortened to about 1 in. so that they form short spurs on which the fruit buds will form (see inset A).

Black currants are treated quite differently. These produce their fruit next year on growth made this year. Therefore, the new side shoots are not cut back. The pruning consists of removing old or unfruitful wood, completely if it has produced no new wood, or partially to a point where new growth starts, as in inset B.

Gooseberries behave in a way that is a combination of the methods of black and red currants. In other words, they bear fruit on short spurs along old branches and on sturdy new growth. We therefore shorten to 1 in. thin, crowded or crossing growths—in the centre of the bush particularly to make picking the fruit less painful. Good leader shoots are shortened by a third and weaker ones by a half. Side shoots that are sturdy are just tipped while weaker ones are cut back to six buds from their point of origin. When dealing with old bushes cut out the oldest wood each year to get new replacement. See inset C.

In all cases try to keep the centre of the bush open so as to achieve a sort of wine glass formation in the shoot arrangement. When all growth can get adequate light and air growth is usually better, fruit production and ripening improved and the possibility of pests and diseases is decreased.

SOFT-FRUIT CUTTINGS

Few of us have sufficient soft fruit for our needs, particularly if we have a deep freeze, since all the surplus can be so easily preserved for use later on when they are unobtainable in the shops—or the price is prohibitive.

Now is the time to remedy that situation by increasing our stock of bushes. This is easily done by rooting cuttings.

Let's start with gooseberries. The pieces you need are shoots produced this year. Cut off the top of the shoot, about 1 ft. long, or pull off the entire shoot with a "heel" of the old wood attached if it isn't longer than 1 ft. The top of the shoot, an inch or so of the softest growth, is removed as well as all the thorns and buds except the top 3 or 4, as shown in inset A.

The cuttings are set in a 6 in. deep trench, about 6 in. apart in the row. If your soil is heavy put plenty of sand in the bottom, otherwise no preparation is needed.

Dip each cutting in hormone rooting powder, place in position in the trench, only the retained buds being above ground level, fill in the soil and press down firmly with a foot.

Red currant cuttings are prepared and planted in the same way, except that 4 or 5 buds are retained, see inset C.

With black currants there are differences. All buds are retained and the cuttings are planted rather deeper, so that only 2 or 3 buds are above ground level—see inset B.

The reason for this is that we want gooseberries and red currants to make bushes based on a short leg or main stem, while we want black currants to make growth from below ground level. This is due to the difference in their fruiting habit, as black currants fruit on the previous season's growth, while the others fruit on spurs at the base of the current year's growth.

There is also a difference when it comes to transplanting the new stock. Black currants can be transferred next autumn, the others not until the autumn after that.

PLANTING EVERGREENS

The best period for the planting of conifers is November to March in most places. An exception to that rule could wisely be made in those areas where the soil is very heavy. Plant in spring.

Most gardens could be improved by the judicious use of some conifers, if they are chosen wisely, either for their distinctive shape or for colour of foliage. Two distinctive ones are shown. Inset B is THUYA ORIENTALIS SEMPERAUREA and C is T. PLICATA ZEBRINA.

As conifers are permanent plantings, thorough preparation of each site is important and well worth-while in the long run.

Take out a hole wider than the container in which the conifer arrives by about 6 in. each side. Into the second spit of soil at the bottom of the hole dig some well-rotted compost. This is better than manure unless the manure is very old and well-rotted down as we do not want to stimulate the plant into soft new growth until the winter has passed. If the soil is on the heavy side mix in some sand as well.

The plants should be watered before being removed from the containers and the hole as well, if necessary, when it has been prepared. Make sure you plant at the right depth—the soil mark on the main stem shows where the soil level should be when the job is finished. The space between the root ball and the sides of the hole should be filled with a nice friable mixture of good loam and leaf-mould or peat as in inset A. When all has been pressed in nice and firm with a carefully-used foot, give a final watering if the weather is dry.

If the conifers you are planting are sufficiently tall to need support before they are firmly rooted in their new positions, drive in a stake well outside the original root ball, so that you do not harm the roots. And place the stake on the side from which the prevailing wind blows in your area.

Finally, if the root ball is found to be wrapped in sacking do not remove it. The sacking will eventually rot, the roots can grow through it and retaining it minimises root disturbance while planting.

MORE EVERGREEN SUGGESTIONS

I make no apology for returning to the subject of evergreens this week as I want to deal with an entirely different aspect of the matter. In passing, I would like to recommend readers with hedges to emulate the gentleman in the illustration and give their hedges a final trim.

My main purpose this week is to suggest evergreens to use for a special purpose—screening. By a careful study of a good catalogue one can find evergreens not very commonly grown that far surpass those that are frequently seen.

For example, Ivy. The very name produces revulsion in many people. But give it its botanical name, Hedera, and interest is immediately aroused as many people grow attractive forms of Hedera as house-plants.

Where one wants a permanent, all-the-year-round screen an evergreen is obviously better than a deciduous one. Hedera is one of the hardiest, is self-clinging, will withstand clipping and will not harm brick- or stone-work provided the structure is sound. It doesn't need to be the dull green usually seen. H. helix "Jubilee", shown in inset A, has small, dainty, silver and green leaves, H.h. "Buttercup" even has small golden leaves, while H. canariensis "Variegata" has silver and green leaves edged with white and its older leaves become flecked with crimson.

Inset B shows another plant that makes a perfect screen, Magnolia grandiflora. Its polished evergreen leaves are a splendid foil for the large cream flowers (up to 8 in. across) which are richly scented. New growth needs to be tied to supports but it is well worth the trouble as a permanent screen that flowers.

Other splendid plants to grow against walls are to be found in the Viburnum family. One, V. tinus (Laurustinus), is shown in inset C. This is one of the few *winter*-flowering evergreens, and happily it's one of the easiest to grow. The buds are tinted pink and open into flat, white, lacy flower-heads which may span a period from about October to March. Sun or shade, it doesn't mind. Its berries are an added attraction, turning from blue to black.

SCHIZANTHUS

Undoubtedly one of the best pot plants for the cool greenhouse is the Schizanthus. It is one of the easiest to grow, doesn't need any more heat than is necessary to exclude frost during the winter, and, grown under such cool conditions, will produce robust plants eventually smothered in flowers.

It is also called the Butterfly Flower or Poor Man's Orchid and the flowers do, to some extent, resemble miniature orchids. The colours range from a pinkish white to pink, rose and crimson, many with contrasting golden centres.

Sown now they should be in bloom in early spring but here again they are most accommodating as they can be had in flower at almost any time, this being determined by when they are sown.

Any good sowing medium can be used, the John Innes one, a soilless one, or one made up yourself from a mixture of equal parts of good loam, peat and sand.

Fill the seed-box and sprinkle the seed sparingly on the top. Cover the seed lightly with silver sand and keep covered with a sheet of glass and brown paper until germination.

If you have a propagating frame, pop them in that. When they are large enough to handle, they should be pricked out.

For indoor flowering, a good plan is to put four or five in each 5 or 6 in. pot. When they are established, the tops should be nipped out to make them produce bushy plants. They may need stopping in this way more than once.

There are several forms to choose from. Perhaps the best for size of flowers and diversity of colours is one called Butterfly, shown in inset A, which will form bushy plants from 1½ to 2½ ft. high. At the other end of the scale is Hit Parade, as in inset B, which is only 1 ft. high but has, perhaps, more striking flowers in the contrast between the basic colour and the centre. Another popular variety is the Pansy-flowered type which has more rounded flowers, self-coloured from pale blue to deep purple.

CABBAGES

After the dog, the humble cabbage is probably man's next best friend. In its various forms it can undoubtedly provide us with a goodly proportion of our regular food and, despite the poor reputation it has with some people, it can be very tasty if properly grown and properly cooked.

So far as growing is concerned, provided it is given good soil that does not get waterlogged in winter, on a site sheltered from the prevailing wind, the final product will be tender to eat.

It also pays to be selective with the actual plants, whether you have grown your own or you are buying them. Lift plants carefully with a fork when the soil is moist to avoid breaking the fine roots. Reject any that do not come up to the standard of the plant shown in inset A. This means having a short, sturdy stem with a good spread of leaves and a compact ball of roots on which as much soil as possible is retained.

They should be planted about 9 in. apart in rows twice that distance apart. Sprinkle each hole before planting with Calomel dust, to avoid club-root disease, and plant with a dibber or trowel handle to make each plant really firm in the ground, as shown in inset B.

Some people may wonder why they are set out only 9 in. apart in the row. The reason for this is to get a double supply of usable vegetables from the one crop, as it were. In early spring you can take out alternate plants for use as spring greens and leave the others in to make good hearts for use later on.

If, at the time when you are considering using some as spring greens, you find that a really hard winter has retarded their growth give all the plants a dressing of sulphate of ammonia, about an ounce to the square yard. In a couple of weeks or so this will have stimulated them into fine new growth that will be really tender when cooked and the flavour may well surprise you. But don't be tempted to apply the stimulant too soon, before the weather has started to improve, or you will produce soft, sappy growth that may well suffer in a subsequent frost.

CHINESE GOOSEBERRIES

"Have you ever heard of Chinese Gooseberries and how do you grow them?" asks a reader. Well, I have heard of them but I have never grown them. I have seen them growing at Ardingly in Sussex, where Kew Gardens have a country branch, as it were. I find that plants are available from specialist nurseries and even seeds from one establishment.

The proper name is Actinidia chinensis and it is more commonly grown as a vigorous, hardy, self-supporting climber for covering pergolas and fences rather than for its fruit but, of course, it has the advantage over many climbers of being dual-purpose.

So why not try it if you have a large area to cover? It grows rapidly and will attain a spread if allowed to, of some 30 ft. But if you want it to cover a somewhat smaller space and you want it mainly as a fruit producer then it must be spur-pruned—that is, all side shoots should be cut back to three buds to make fruiting spurs in winter.

All it needs to thrive is medium, rich soil but the drainage should be good. The leaves at first are a reddish shade but later on are a bright green. It produces, in July and August, cup-shaped, creamy, fragrant flowers, male on some plants and female on others, so you will need at least one of each sex for fertilisation to get any fruit. All parts, except the flowers, are hairy and a south or west aspect suits it best.

The fruit (shown in the insets) are usually about 2 in. long and the downy skins are removed—they turn brown when they are ripe—in order to eat the flesh inside. It has a flavour all its own. I have seen it described as a cross between greengage and grape and that is about the most accurate description for it in the opinion of the growers. As the fruit appears rather late in the year you may have to finish ripening some indoors, as we do with outdoor tomatoes.

As with most climbers, the planting season extends from October to March. Seed would be sown in a cold frame in April. Shoots can be layered in November and cuttings can then be placed in a cold frame, using pieces of half-ripened shoots.

HAZELNUTS—GROW A HEDGE TO EAT

ONE OF the special joys of the countryside in February are the golden yellow catkins of the hazel, swaying backwards and forwards with every breath of wind. Hazels can reach the proportions of a small tree, but, by and large, in the copses, valleys, and hedgerows up and down the country they remain what one would describe as large shrubs.

They are shrubs which are well suited to growing in Britain.

In the whole wide world there are only 15 different kinds of hazel and all of them are native to the Northern Hemisphere and in particular to Europe.

There are two distinct types of hazel nut in Britain: cob-nuts and filberts.

Cob-nuts, which are so common in the North of England and in Scotland, are distinguished from the other kind by their toothed husks which cover the upper half of the oval nuts.

Filberts, on the other hand, can be instantly recognised by the fact that the large heart-shaped nuts are entirely covered with a flask-like husk.

That word filbert comes from the French *noix de filbert*. For in France such nuts are ripe about St. Philibert's day (August 22). Although in the parts of southern England where they are generally grown commercially, they are not ready before the middle of September.

In fact both kinds of hazel produce good-sized, well-flavoured nuts when grown commercially—or in your garden.

Hazels make a useful as well as an attractive addition to any garden. You can plant them singly, in which case they will grow slowly to about 10 ft. Or you can plant them 2 ft. apart to form in time a thick 5 ft. high hedge.

Imagine a hedge that not only acts as a screen and windbreak but also produces tasty fruit. Well, that's the hazel.

If your choice is a single shrub by itself, then there are several possibilities open to you.

You can choose your shrub primarily for the beauty of its contorted branches and its springtime catkins, or you can grow a hazel mainly for its nuts.

You can have the slow-growing Corkscrew Hazel with its curiously twisted branches which have a definite eye-appeal in winter. Some people may know this shrub as Harry Lauder's Walking Stick. One look at the branches will tell you why.

You can also have a yellow-leaved form of hazel called Aurea. It makes a splendid foil for green and purple leaved shrubs in summer.

All hazels incidentally produce fine autumnal tints. This has little to do with wind or frost. It is simply that the leaves contain carotene and xanthophyll, nature's chemical time-fuse compounds which ensure the shrubs do lose their leaves in autumn.

Both the Corkscrew and Yellow Hazels bear yellow catkins, often up to 2½ in. long, and later clusters of cob-nuts.

Each nut tree should bear fruit on its own. For all hazels have male and female catkins. The females are so tiny that they are barely noticeable.

Pollination, as with so many British trees and grasses, is carried out by the wind. The chances of any one pollen grain reaching a female catkin are remote. So much more pollen is produced than is actually necessary. This strangely wasteful method of pollination is also inefficient and the reason why some nut bushes fail to bear fruit.

So, if you can, plant two shrubs, preferably with one behind the other in the direction of the prevailing wind which in spring is from the South West.

The "filbert" hazel also makes an attractive small tree for the garden.

There is a variety called the Purple-leafed Filbert which has oval, deep purple foliage and looks truly magnificent beside trees, shrubs, and plants with leaves of lighter colours. Even the copper beech cannot compare with this hazel's leaves.

You could plant the Purple-leafed Filbert near (about 10 ft.) the yellow-leafed cob-nut Aurea, for an excellent contrast, which not only will give your garden visual impact but will make doubly certain that you will be able to collect nuts in September and October.

If you want to be really certain of the best possible crop, I suggest that you plant Lambert Filbert with Pearson's Dwarf Prolific to ensure good pollination. You could perhaps have six Lamberts in a hedge to every Pearson.

The nuts of Lambert Filbert are large, glossy, and superbly flavoured when ripe. This is the variety which is most commonly grown commercially in this country.

Nut bushes can be planted between November and March—though the sooner the better. Any well-drained soil is suitable, and you can plant in either sun or shade.

To get the best from your bushes a little initial pruning is necessary. After planting cut back the previous year's growth by half to encourage plenty of twiggy fruit-producing shoots.

With a nut hedge if you cut back old growths in March annually after flowering, then not only will the hedge be kept tidy, but it will also be certain to bear a good crop.

Nut trees attract two pests. The first is the grey squirrel, so destructive in any woodland area, and the second is the nut weevil which bores holes in shells, eats the kernels, and causes secondary attacks by brown rot fungus.

You can do little about the squirrels but if you spray your bushes with Fentro in early June you will have no weevil problem.

A nut bush brightens the garden from February with its catkins, soothes the eye with its green leaves in spring and summer, and holds the promise of nuts and golden leaves in autumn. Even in winter those bleak branches are decorative when the garden takes on the harsh form of a wind blasted heath.

If you had a little nut tree, much pleasure would it bear.

ROSE CARE

As prevention is better than cure, the possibility of rose troubles next year can be minimised by taking certain steps as soon as your rose-trees are completely dormant—usually towards the end of this month, depending on the weather.

The first step is a thorough clean up of the bed as well as the plants. Cut off all dead wood, and prune the bushes lightly. Inset A shows an example of before and after this treatment.

Pick up all the cuttings and all fallen leaves. This is particularly important if you have suffered from black spot during the summer. The appearance of leaves affected with black spot is shown in inset B. If such leaves are left on the ground the black spot spores will spend the winter in the soil of the bed, ready to attack again next year. Also *pull* up all weeds. Burn all this debris, to ensure destruction of disease.

Having got the plants and the bed properly clean, another good step is to spray the plants as a precaution against the carrying over of disease. Use Bordeaux mixture or copper sulphate at a strength of one ounce in a gallon of water.

If you use copper sulphate mix it in a plastic container, not a metal one as it will corrode metal. And for this reason be very particular to clean your spray thoroughly afterwards or the metal parts may be harmed by corrosion.

When this has been done, make sure that every bush is really firm in the soil. Frost and wind tend to loosen them and this is probably the reason why more rose trees are lost during the winter than any other. This is another reason for the pruning, as it lessens the wind resistance of the bush, so that it does not get blown back and forth.

Finally, if you have some well-rotted manure or compost, give the bed a good mulch—two or three inches thick. You'll see the benefit of this in the way your plants respond in the spring.

As soon as the first signs of growth are seen, do your pruning proper—from mid March in southern England to early April in northern Scotland.

OUTDOOR CROP PROTECTION

To me, one of the saddest sights in a garden in wintertime is a desolate scene where vegetable crops have been allowed to spoil or go to waste for want of a little care.

Several members of the brassica (cabbage) family are liable to suffer in this way. The humble cabbage, for example, can be blown over and then, perhaps, buried in snow so that it starts to rot. To prevent this, earth up the cabbages (as one does potatoes) right up to the bottom leaves. This not only keeps them upright but also makes an effective drainage channel between the rows.

Brussels Sprouts should be similarly supported but as these plants are so much taller they also need a firm stake to which each plant is tied.

Winter cauliflowers (which we used to call Broccoli) should have a spadeful of earth taken from the north side of the plant, see inset A. The plant should then be pushed over to the north and the soil placed on the south side. The curds, which frost may discolour, should also be protected by the leaves, the main rib of the leaf being broken, if necessary, to make it lie over the curds.

Celery is another crop that should be protected. Cover it with straw (if you can get it) bracken or similar light plant refuse. Then place over the row two boards nailed together, as shown in inset B, to act as a watershed so that rain or snow does not lie in the crowns and cause rot to set in.

Some root crops, such as parsnips, do not really need lifting. Frost improves the flavour anyway. But if your land is heavy, and lifting them out of thick mud is never a very pleasant job, take up enough to use for a week or two when the weather and soil are suitable and store them in a box in the garden shed. Cover them with peat or sand, as shown in inset C, and they will come to no harm. This also avoids the problem that if the ground becomes frozen solid, lifting some parsnips for immediate use may be well-nigh impossible. Another way of preventing this problem arising is to cover the row deeply with garden refuse, thus preventing the soil freezing.

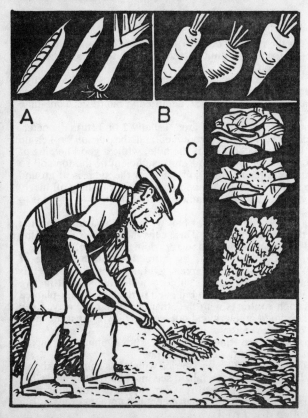

A

B

C

SOIL CONDITIONING

One of the basic rules of gardening is that you cannot expect to produce good crops without good husbandry. In other words, you must do all you can to improve the condition, texture and fertility of your soil. To the beginner, this may seem a formidable task. But it is not really difficult to effect considerable improvement in most soils, provided you can supply the requisite energy, over a period of time.

Digging, of course, is the basis of the procedure. Get all the vacant land turned over during the cold weather when the land is dry enough to tread on without it caking. Leave it in large lumps as turned up by the fork. The frost will do an excellent job on it for you and in the spring you will find it breaks down into a fine top tilth quite easily.

At the same time, dig into it all the manure, peat, rotting vegetation, grass, etc., you can. This will rot down and provide humus which is what most soils need. Light sandy soil needs it particularly to improve its moisture-retaining properties, while on heavy land or clay the humus helps to make it more workable. In all soils the humus will also increase the amount of food available to plant roots later on.

If your humus-providing material is limited, dress one third of your vegetable plot with it each year and practise crop rotation. Having done one third, grow onions, peas, beans, leeks, etc. (inset A) on that part the first year. Then root crops, as in inset B, the second year and then cabbages, etc. (C) the third year. The second year, manure the second part and make the crop order C,A,B. The third year manure the remainder and make the crop order B,C,A. Thus the crops in A are always grown on the newly manured section, those in B on the part manured the previous year and those in C on the part manured two years earlier.

Crop rotation is beneficial not only to the vegetables grown but also to the land itself as its fertility is regularly maintained by this process.

Some land can be further improved by lime but apply it, if necessary, in spring, not at the same time as manure. Soil test kits can be bought quite cheaply to show whether lime is needed on your ground.

SHRUBS FOR COLOUR

The best period for the planting of trees and shrubs, both evergreen and deciduous, extends from now until March, so choose a time when the soil is in good condition.

More and more people are planting these subjects as their attractive appearance is equalled by their labour-saving virtue.

Some hard work is necessary at first, admittedly, but this is a one-time effort that is well worth while.

For each plant a hole adequate in area, usually 2 or 3 ft. in diameter, should be dug out. The top soil is removed and the subsoil broken up with a fork but kept at the bottom of the hole, while a good helping of manure, compost, etc., is mixed in. Return sufficient of the top soil so that when the shrub is planted the soil mark on the stem is at ground level. Add more soil over the roots and tread well in, finishing off nicely level after finally treading down. Firmness is important, as frost tends to lift the soil.

If your plants arrive with the root ball wrapped in sacking, cut the string but leave the sacking in place. This keeps the ball of soil round the roots intact and the sacking will soon rot, doing no harm.

I have in the past written about the attractions of the foliage of evergreens in its varying shades of green, gold, silver and blue, so this time I am suggesting a few deciduous subjects which are very attractive in their autumnal attire on their own but even better when inter-planted with conifers as each contrasts with the other in a delightful way. Even in the summer their vivid greens stand out wonderfully against the more sombre shades of the evergreens.

Outstanding examples are Rhus cotinoides, Rhus typhina, the Japanese maples, Fothergilla monticola, and so on.

One you shouldn't omit is Cornus sibirica which has shiny red shoots after its brilliantly red leaves have fallen, see inset B. If your house has white or cream-coloured walls, inset A is for you. It is Vitis amurensis. Against such a background, its summer green and autumn crimson is a never-to-be-forgotten display.

APPLE STORING

The way apples are picked and stored makes all the difference to your chances of keeping the fruit in sound condition right through the winter. Choose a dry day if you can to pick the fruit and not too early in the day so that the dew has had a chance to dry off.

The fruit must be fully mature. To test this lift up one apple. It should come off the tree very easily. Then cut it in half. If the pips are brown the fruit is ready for harvesting.

Pick carefully and *place* each one in the container—don't drop it in as a bruised apple will not keep. Every fruit should be examined individually and any malformed or damaged fruit kept apart for immediate use. In other words, store only perfect, full-size fruit.

Each eating apple should be wrapped as shown in inset A. Cooking apples need not be wrapped. In both cases they should be placed side by side in a single layer in a box, making sure that the cookers do not touch each other—see inset B. The best boxes to use are those with little wooden posts, higher than the sides, at each corner. These are usually called Dutch trays and can often be obtained from a greengrocer. The advantage of the high corners is that the boxes can be stored one on top of another without the one above touching the fruit in the one below, as in inset C.

The ideal place to store apples is one with a moist atmosphere and a temperature of about 37-40°F. (3-4°C.). The cellars of old houses were ideal but not many of us have cellars nowadays. The spare room would probably be all right but not in a centrally-heated house. The attic might do if it isn't too cold but the best place would probably be a garage or well-built garden shed, provided it is rat and mouse free.

For the first month leave the boxes of fruit uncovered as they give off a lot of moisture to begin with, particularly in damp weather. After that cover them with black polythene or sacking to exclude light, but don't tuck it round them snugly as they need plenty of air.

Inspect the fruit regularly and immediately remove any showing signs of decay before it can infect the others.

FORCING RHUBARB

Nothing seems to give most gardeners more pleasure than the production of a crop out of season—or should I say earlier than their friends' or neighbours'? Which is why, I suppose, forcing rhubarb is so popular.

If you have a heated greenhouse you could probably get enough nice pink sticks for use at Christmas by acting now. The root to force should be dug up and left on the surface of the ground for about a week to get frosted—see inset A. This retardation seems to spur the plant into superhuman efforts once it gets inside. The frost apparently increases the sugar available in the plant and thus produces more tasty sticks.

Place the root in a box of really good soil or plant it in a similar medium in the ground under the greenhouse staging. Water well and cover with black polythene or something similar to exclude light.

Similar procedure is followed for forcing out of doors, except that the root is replanted in a specially-prepared spot, as sheltered as possible, in which a heavy dressing of well-rotted manure has been dug into the second spit. The crown is planted at the same level as when it was dug up but after re-planting give it a good mulch of strawy manure. Then cover it with a bucket, half barrel or something similar (insets B and C). Heap over this cover as much strawy manure, compost, leaves or even grass-cuttings as you can to engender some warmth.

Out of doors, of course, it will not produce those nice pink sticks as early as when it is forced in a greenhouse but it will still be considerably earlier than that grown naturally.

Those plants forced in this way in the garden can be left where they are for future crops but roots forced in a greenhouse will have to be sacrificed for they will not be any use afterwards.

The roots forced in the garden should be allowed to rest afterwards—in other words don't pull sticks from them, after you have taken the early crop, for the remainder of the year. Sacrificing the greenhouse-forced roots may seem a pity but stock can easily be increased by dividing clumps in the garden between November and February.

WINTER CARE

When we are promised, or should I say threatened, with a severe winter, the care of plants in a greenhouse or cold frame assumes greater importance to avoid losses.

Watering plays a very important part in this care. Do not leave cans or buckets of water in the greenhouse during severe weather, as one normally does in the summer time. The presence of such water increases the moisture content in the air in the house at a time when we want to keep the atmosphere as dry as possible.

Give the pot plants only a little water at a time, as the drier the soil, the less likely it is to freeze. In very severe weather you can probably withhold water altogether.

Always mop up any water spilt on the staging or floor as a damp atmosphere is an encouragement to problems such as mildew and mould. It is also wise to use tepid water rather than cold.

To keep the atmosphere buoyant, as we call it, give the greenhouse or frame some ventilation during a suitable period of the day, even if it is only for half-an-hour. Inset A shows a very useful little gadget for regulating the ventilation of a frame. It is just a piece of wood of a suitable size cut into a stepped shape as shown so that the frame light can be raised to different heights, in accordance with the weather.

In the greenhouse, of course, you can similarly regulate the ventilation by the amount you open the window. Use a top window, on the side away from the wind.

If you do get a pot plant's soil frozen don't plunge it into hot water to thaw it out, as I have known people do, as that will almost certainly kill the plant. Plunge it into a bucket of cold water, as shown in inset B. Also sprinkle the foliage with cold water and then stand the pot in a cool place that is properly frostproof. And don't stand it in sunshine, if we have any, as that would be just as bad as the hot water treatment. When the plant has thawed out, move it into a warmer atmosphere. It will probably be several hours before it has completely thawed out naturally so don't be in too much of a hurry to transfer it to a warmer place.

PEAS AND BROAD BEANS

Vegetable production is so important nowadays to the average household budget that we should make a start as soon as possible to obtain crops for the kitchen as early in the new year as one can.

Two of the earliest subjects are peas and broad beans, which we can sow now this month. Peas are the more important, as not everyone likes broad beans and these in any case are rather uncertain when sown in November in northern districts.

So, first of all, the peas. You need a first early, round-seeded sort, such as Forward, Meteor or Superb. Why round-seeded, I have often been asked. The reason, apart from hardiness, is that the rain readily runs off a round, smooth-skinned seed. With the other kind, the wrinkled-seeded varieties, the water can lie in the wrinkles and thus start the seed rotting before it has time to grow.

For these November sowings, light ground is best, preferably dug two spits deep and manured for a previous crop. Draw a drill about 3 in. deep and 6 in. wide with the flat side of a hoe. If your soil is not really light make the drill only 2 in. in depth. Place the seed as shown in inset A, 2 or 3 in. apart in a treble row. If you can give them cloche protection so much the better but this is not essential in most areas. If you do use cloches make sure you securely block each end, as shown in inset B, as otherwise the cloches become a wind tunnel and do more harm than good.

For broad beans, choose the most sheltered and therefore the warmest spot you can. The drill should again be a flat one, 9 in. wide and 3 in. deep. The seeds are sown in a double row, 9 in. apart each way. Cloches are also an advantage for this crop. You need a variety such as Giant Seville or Aquadulce Claudia. When these plants are in full flower, pinch out the tops. This helps to produce an early crop with better-filled pods, as well as being a good way to avoid an attack of black-fly (to which they are very prone) as the fly prefers (naturally) the soft, juicy young growth at the top of the plant.

GREENHOUSES—YOUR OWN TROPICAL ISLE

IMAGINE IF you could leave the fog and the frost, the drizzle and the dreariness of a British winter behind and set up a garden on some sub-tropical isle. . . .

Just think of being able to have a predictable climate where one warm day followed another . . . where the sun's heat coaxed the frailest seedling into vigorous growth.

An island where you could grow almost any plant which took your fancy.

Yet, did you know that you could have your very own little tropical isle—in your back garden?

All you have to do is to put a tiny part of it under glass and it is marvellous what you can achieve.

Come, let me show you. Let us explore together the possibilities of a greenhouse, where you could garden indoors in winter.

In a greenhouse you can grow exotic plants such as alpines from Mexico, orchids, cacti and an ever-changing selection of plants for indoor decoration. You could grow Christmas flowering chrysanthemums, or specialise in carnations so that you have a "button-hole" all year. You can raise many half-hardy annuals from seed such as antirrhinums, nemesia, petunias, salvias, verbena and zinnias, and for a few pence fill your garden with the scent and colour of summer.

There is also the attraction of having fresh lettuce in winter; cucumbers, tomatoes and melons in summer; and a place to give vegetables like cauliflowers a good start to life before planting them outside in late spring.

And with some of the latest greenhouse equipment to help you there is no reason why any of your efforts should not be successful.

There are four types of greenhouses which can make all these things possible. They are known as cold, cool, warm or hot houses, according to how much heat, if any, is provided.

A cold house has no heating, but it is ideal for growing all kinds of alpine plants throughout a wet British winter. In addition you can grow perpetual flowering carnations, and all kinds of bulbs in pots; you can raise vegetables in boxes for transplating later to the garden and you can grow tomatoes in "ring" pots or Gro-Bags from plants bought in April, or from plants raised in the warmth of your kitchen.

A cool house usually affords a minimum winter temperature of 45°F. In it you can grow many exotic plants, including orchids and cacti.

Then there are all sorts of flowering and foliage pot plants such as begonias, calceolaria, cineraria, coleus, cyclamen, geraniums, primulas which will provide colour all year round. You can take your pick of the vegetables you wish to grow in addition to honeydew melons, peppers, aubergines and tomatoes.

By putting specially grown bush fruit trees in large pots,

you can have plums, cherries, peaches and nectarines in parts of Britain where the cultivation of these fruits outdoors is impossible.

The true warm and hot houses have minimum winter night temperatures of 50°F. to 60°F. and are really only necessary for a few tropical plants. With the ever-increasing price of fuel, such temperatures can only be attempted in the South and those parts of the West of England, Wales, Ireland and Scotland warmed by the Gulf Stream.

What size of greenhouse should you have? I consider that one 8ft. by 8ft. is about the minimum size for general use, although one measuring 10ft. by 8ft. and costing little more, is a better investment.

Some greenhouses with wooden frames can be chosen with either or both lower halves of the house made of boards, which enables you to suit your greenhouse to your intended plants. For example, you could grow pot plants on the boarded side and grow tomatoes and later chrysanthemums on the glass to ground side.

The latest aluminium greenhouses are an excellent buy and they will provide endless years of service and enjoyment with little or no maintenance costs.

Provided that plenty of light is available, the greenhouse should be as near to the house as possible so that you can more easily provide water, gas and electricity.

Now let us suppose that you have made up your mind about the type of greenhouse you want. Your next considerations should be the growing conditions of the plants—the fresh air supply, humidity, light and shade and, more important, adequate heat.

So let us start with heating. Electricity is very expensive, but thermostatically controlled tubular heaters and fan heaters may be the answer for small greenhouses for short periods in spring to enable tender plants to be grown.

If you require such heat to raise seeds, why not have an electric propagator in your greenhouse with soil warming cables? It is very much cheaper to run.

Next there is natural gas. The actual heater, which can also be fuelled by bottled propane, is fairly expensive to buy and to install, but it has the cheapest of all running costs.

However, still the simplest and most popular method of heating is by using a paraffin heater coupled to a large fuel storage drum to give continuous heating for a week or more.

Now what about ventilation? For in summer the sun can send the temperature in a small greenhouse soaring. A greenhouse, 8ft. × 8ft., should have two ventilators on each side of the roof and, if possible, a louvred ventilator low down on one of the walls.

Then there is the need for a proper humid atmosphere especially for orchids and pot plants. This can be achieved by standing them in trays of moistened gravel. But for more vigorous plants like tomatoes, you can take the worry out of watering when you are on holiday by installing an automatic system.

And should the sun beat down too fiercely on your "tropical isle," you can put up attractive PVC shades on the sunny side of the house.

Conversely in chill winter when you want to preserve as much of your valuable heat as possible, the answer is to "triple-glaze" with quilted polythene.

GROUNDWORK

Though there are several "no-digging" schools of thought, I still believe that the best basis for successful gardening is good cultivation by fork or spade. This is the ideal time of year for this sort of work, provided the condition of the soil is suitable. On light land this is not so much of a problem but on heavier ground one has to choose one's time more carefully. But it is wise to do it as soon as you can because the more time the frost has to work on upturned soil the better the texture will be next year.

This is, I admit, hard work. Unless you are the young, husky, rugger-playing type, you should not do too much in one spell. Get your body used to this form of exercise gradually.

The purpose of the exercise is to get the top soil exposed to the severe weather so that many of the harmful insects and weed seeds are killed by being exposed. Secondly, the sub-soil, or second spit, is dug over to break it up and thus improve drainage as well as to make it much easier for plant roots next year to penetrate deeper, thus keeping their tips in moist soil, the best possible answer to the drying out of the top soil in a dry summer.

In order to encourage this and to increase the amount of nourishment they will obtain at that level, spread a layer of manure, compost or some similar humus-producing material along the bottom of each trench before turning over the bottom with a fork. This will have decomposed by next year and will be an excellent medium for promoting root growth, for retaining moisture and for supplying plant food.

Of course, it would be ideal if you could dig over in this way your entire plot—even where you may plan to have a lawn—but if this is impossible, dig individual trenches in this way. In these you can grow those subjects which benefit most from this process, such as runner beans, sweet-peas, parsnips, etc. If you have never seen the way dahlias respond when planted in ground worked in this way you could be in for a pleasant surprise next year.

PLANT PROTECTION

There are several simple ways in which those plants you are particularly fond of and therefore do not wish to risk losing can be protected from the worst of the winter's severity.

Once the old, tall growth has been cut down almost to ground level on such favourites as paeonies, delphiniums, carnations, etc., cover the crowns with light strawy manure, bracken or twiggy garden refuse. This acts as a surprisingly effective shield against frost and cold wind.

Subjects such as pampas grass or red-hot poker should have their tall foliage and stems twisted together and tied round with twine.

Small shrubs, especially newly-planted ones, can be protected as shown in inset A, by making a screen of polythene secure to uprights and placing this round them on the windward side. An even more effective shield is shown in inset C. This consists of canes pushed into the ground around the chosen subjects, brought together at the top and firmly secured in that position with twine. Over this framework a sheet of polythene is fitted quite tightly, the bottom being anchored down by bricks or stones.

Clear polythene is best as it admits light and does not get saturated as sacking would. Although dry sacking would probably be more of a barrier to the cold, once it gets wet its weight is a definite disadvantage.

Covers of this kind should not be left in place any longer than is really necessary as if they are they may induce the plant into premature growth which would be very soft and very susceptible to damage from subsequent frost.

Another advantage of polythene over sacking or fabric of that kind is that snow tends to slide off polythene but to remain in place on material while its weight may well bear down on the foliage underneath.

There are many rock plants which dislike being saturated, particularly those with downy leaves which hold water and snow for long periods and which may then freeze. These should have a "roof" placed over them, as shown in inset B. This is merely a piece of glass supported on suitably shaped wires. It should be slightly sloped so that rain and snow run off.

CHRYSANTHEMUMS

As soon as your indoor chrysanthemums have finished flowering, the main stems should be cut down to about 6 in. of the soil surface. If any of the plants have already made shoots about 6 in. long these should be removed as they will be of soft, sappy growth that will be no use for cuttings.

If you plan to start taking cuttings from these old stools in January, the soil in the pots should be lightly broken up with a knife or piece of wood to a depth of about an inch—not deeper or you'll be breaking up the roots.

The pots should then be stood on the staging near the glass in full light. They should also be watered to prompt them into producing new shoots. If you can add to the water some soot and liquid manure so much the better. Keep them just nicely moist, watering them probably once a week.

They should also be sprayed with nicotine or some similar insecticide as aphis show remarkable reproductive ability in a warm house even in winter. In fact, a thorough spraying or fumigating of the whole house at this time is a wise precaution to safeguard not only the chrysanthemums but all the other plants you may have there. And don't be satisfied that once you've done it all is well. It may well need doing several times during the winter.

Outdoor chrysanths should also be tucked up for the winter. Many of these will safely winter where they are but one usually finds that the best varieties are not as hardy as their forebears. So those you particularly like should be dug up and the stools packed side by side (carefully labelled) in boxes 4 or 5 inches deep. Any spaces between or around the stools should be filled by sprinkling nicely moist soil mixed with peat (equal parts) all over the box so that the surface is up to the level of the base of the stems.

Water and spray as before and place the boxes in a cold-frame for the winter. Keep the light closed and cover with mats or sacking during very severe weather. Remove this when the weather eases.

INDOOR PLANTS

At this time of year a few urgent jobs to do in the greenhouse is more than sufficient excuse to get inside out of the cold. But surprisingly few people seem to realise that we can, in fact, make a start now in the greenhouse (a heated one, of course) in the production of food crops.

Have you, for example, ever tried sowing early peas in boxes or pots in the greenhouse at this time of year? Use a mixture of 2 parts of loam to 1 each of silver sand and peat or leaf-mould. Space the peas out carefully, 2 in. apart each way in a box or round the edge of a good-sized pot. Water moderately at first until they have germinated, then spray lightly each day. When the seedlings are 5 or 6 in. high, give them a boost by sprinkling between them a light dressing of equal parts of fine loam and old, powdered manure. Dwarf French beans can be treated in the same way to produce really early crops. And what about sowing a few carrots, lettuces, onions and leeks, mustard and cress, and even tomatoes?

Before I am accused of thinking too much about my stomach, let me give you a useful tip about preventing the ill-effect of fog in a greenhouse, which frequently results in damping-off. This can be avoided, during foggy weather, by standing one or two pint jars of water in the greenhouse, among the plants, after adding to each jar two teaspoonfuls of ammonia. Remove the jars as soon as the fog has cleared.

A facet of greenhouse gardening that is very interesting (and one that pleases the ladies no end) is to bring inside a few plants to pot and force into flower very early. It may surprise you how many respond to this treatment. Primroses, polyanthus, primulas, lily-of-the-valley, violas and pansies, many kinds of bulbs, shrubs such as heathers—the list is almost endless. Try some you don't think will respond, just to see if you can succeed in inducing them to do so. If you do succeed you'll find it very satisfying—you can get the wife to buy you a bigger hat for Christmas!

HOT-BED

With the ever-increasing popularity of riding, horse-manure is more readily available to gardeners in many areas nowadays. This means that those without a heated greenhouse can still raise early crops of carrots, lettuces, etc., by making a hot-bed and placing a garden frame on top of it.

Having got your manure, as the husband of a famous cook might have said, build it into a mound, wetting any part that seems dry. Leave it for four days, then turn it inside out. Do this two more times at four-day intervals. By this time the first fierce heat will have been dissipated and it is ready for building the hot-bed, which should be a foot wider and longer than the frame to. stand it on.

Place the most strawy part at the bottom and on that place a layer of leaves. Tread each layer reasonably firm. Repeat this process, using a layer of manure, then a layer of leaves, treading firm each one, until you have a heap about two feet deep.

Place the frame in position, as shown in inset A, and in it put a 6 in. layer of good loam and peat, in equal parts, well mixed and sifted to ensure that it is nice and fine.

You can build a hot-bed of manure alone but by mixing in leaves as described the heat is not so great but lasts much longer. Two months is the normal expectation of useful heat from such a bed.

At this stage you really need a soil thermometer because seed should not be sown until the temperature has dropped to 75°F. (24°C.). If you do not have one, push a stick into the bed, right down into the base, not merely into the top soil, and leave it there for ten minutes. Pull it out and if the lower part is not too hot to hold in your hand seed can be sown. If it is too hot leave the bed a few days and try again.

When you sow the seed, broadcast it thinly, as sowing in rows would waste quite a lot of useful space, as shown in inset B.

When the seed has germinated, ventilate the frame occasionally for half an hour or so in suitable weather, particularly if and when the sun shines.

SHALLOTS AND GARLIC

As so many people have difficulty in growing onions satisfactorily, I feel much greater use should be made of shallots. They are so easy to grow that even those people who do grow them seldom give them much attention.

During the growing season admittedly they need no attention, except, perhaps, to keep them weed-free. The real need is for proper preparation of the site. A strip the width of a fork should be dug and a dressing of manure, or some available substitute, dug into the second spit. This ensures that the soil in which they sit will be well-drained and that nourishment will be available when they want it. This preparation could wisely be done now, as soon as the soil is dry enough.

Then when the ground is in a suitable condition, any time between now and the end of February, the little bulbs can be pressed into the surface, 6 in. apart, one row 1 ft. from another, so that only the tips of the bulbs are above the surface. Cut off any long, straggling tips to make it more difficult for birds to pull them up. Worms also have a habit of pushing them out of the ground so look at them occasionally and replace any that have been displaced.

Another member of the onion family can be planted during the same period—garlic. Now we are in the Common Market more and more people seem to like to use garlic in their cooking. Preparation of site is the same but the cloves, as garlic divisions are called (see inset A), are planted 2 in. deep, not on the surface.

If your land is on the heavy side, either place a handful of sand under each clove or make a raised bed, as shown in inset B, so as to improve the drainage. In making such a bed you should ensure that the manure is at least 6 in. below the surface when the bed is finished. If you still want real onions and have difficulty in growing them from seed, you should try onion sets but these are not planted until early in the new year. Great advances have been made in onion sets in recent years and they are well worth growing.

FRUIT CARE

At this time of year, when it is not possible to do much in the garden, our fruit trees could wisely be given some attention. Peach trees, for example, could well be sprayed as a means of preventing leaf-curl, a problem that seems to be becoming more common and widespread each year. Many of these trees are grown against fences or walls, so spray these as well as the bare branches of the tree, and the ground underneath them. Lime sulphur is the stuff to use or a copper-based spray. And spray again in February to make sure because the spray does not remain effective for very long. But this second spray must be applied before the flower buds open. This also applies to nectarines and almonds.

Other fruit trees, such as apple and pear, could well have an application of tar-oil winter wash. Naturally, you should do any pruning necessary before spraying as there is no point in wasting spray on those parts that are to be cut off. Tar-oil wash serves a dual purpose as it kills lichen and moss as well as insects and their eggs. If you have any plants or, perhaps, parts of the lawn under the trees, cover these with newspapers as the spray will badly scorch the foliage if it is left unprotected.

Another job in the fruit garden is to cover fruit bushes such as gooseberries with netting having a small mesh, or with black thread taken back and forth across the bush north to south and east to west. This is a great help in keeping the birds off the bushes so that they do not spoil next year's crop by pecking off the dormant fruit buds. These bushes can also be sprayed with lime sulphur if you have any left over after treating the peach trees.

This is also the time of year to remove any large branches from old fruit trees if this is necessary. The important thing to remember is to make a cut underneath the branch first before sawing it off from above, to prevent the limb falling down and tearing off a swathe of bark from the trunk of the tree. A nice clean cut is desirable and this should be painted to prevent disease entering the wound. Don't use creosote for this.

CHRISTMAS POT PLANTS

So many people receive as Christmas presents beautiful foliage or flowering pot plants that they have not grown before that the festive season is always followed for me by a deluge of letters asking for advice on their care. So keen are their recipients to give the plants all the care they think they need that more plants are killed by kindness, as it were, than by any other single factor.

So, first of all, don't over-water them. The soil needs to be kept nicely moist, not soaking wet. Don't water all the plants as a regular routine. Water only those that need it when by touching the soil you can tell that it is dry enough to need water.

Secondly, don't give them too much heat, particularly during the day and then leave them on a cold window-sill at night where they are in danger of catching a chill. High temperatures, especially in centrally-heated rooms, produce a very dry atmosphere which the plants dislike. The ever-popular azalea indica, for instance, must have a moist atmosphere. As well as keeping its soil constantly moist, place its pot in a larger pot or container and pack the space between the two with moist peat and keep this constantly moist as well.

Similarly, the Christmas Begonia (the Gloire de Lorraine type) shown in inset A needs plenty of *tepid* water and the foliage syringed if it is in a dry atmosphere. This syringing is important for large-leaved foliage plants also. Keep Begonias well away from gas fumes.

Another problem child is the Poinsettia, properly Euphorbia pulcherrima (inset B) whose red bracts at the top make such a strong appeal to most people. If conditions are not right you'll soon know because it will start dropping its leaves. It needs the peat packing treatment, the syringing, and tepid water—sparingly. Water-logged soil is fatal. Needs a well-lit spot but no draught or gas fumes.

Inset C shows Primula obconica which isn't very difficult as long as it is well watered and a little liquid feed added to the water. But don't touch it—it can cause a skin rash.

PIPS AND STONES

Christmas offers us the opportunity of producing some house plants from the pips and stones of fruit that may not normally be available in the home. Why not try some? They may not all succeed but those that do will be a source of great interest to yourself and to your friends.

You can use the pips of oranges, tangerines, grapefruit and lemon, as well as the stones of dates, apricots, peaches and the avocado pear, plus the top section of a pineapple.

John Innes or soil-less compost can be used or you can make up your own of equal parts of good loam, peat and silver sand. Fill some pots with this mixture and push the pips in, about $\frac{1}{2}$ in. deep and an inch apart. Put orange pips into one pot, lemon into another and so on. Label them so that later on you know which is which. Cover each pot with a glass jam jar, or the whole lot with a sheet of glass and stand in a dark, warm place until germination occurs. Make sure you keep the compost nicely moist at all times, never saturated and never dry.

When germination has taken place remove the jars or glass and place the pots in the light. After that, cultivate in the normal way, giving a little weak feed occasionally.

The pineapple top is treated rather differently. The top slice bearing the leaves is allowed to dry out for a few days and is then planted, up to the base of the leaves, in a mixture of peat and silver sand, equal parts, in a propagating case. This is simply a box, of the proportions shown, covered with glass. If you can give it bottom heat so much the better.

When roots have formed, as shown by new growth appearing in the centre of the leaf rosette, pot up in damp John Innes compost. Glass is no longer required. To keep it growing well, weak regular feeding is advisable.

Examples of these plants are shown in the insets. A is a date "palm" and B an orange seedling.

155

DECEMBER   Fourth Week

ARMCHAIR GARDENING

In the present economic conditions vegetable crops are particularly important. This week, therefore, I intend to concentrate on suggestions for new, improved varieties for the kitchen garden. The same principles apply to flowers but these are largely a personal choice which you can easily make from the many excellently illustrated catalogues.

Most people appreciate having a good supply of tomatoes for as long a season as possible from plants grown in a greenhouse as well as in the open garden. Out-of-doors, the great thing is to grow a variety that crops as early as possible so as to get the fruit ripe before our elusive sun departs. One of the best in this respect is Outdoor Girl which usually matures about two weeks before other varieties.

For a greenhouse I suggest Infinity Cross, shown in inset A. In an unheated greenhouse you should get 4 lb. of fruit from each of 4 or 5 trusses, while with heat you should get 6 to 8 lb. of fruit from as many as 8 trusses per plant.

Inset B shows a variety of pea called Recette. The great advantage of this variety is that it produces three pods per stem. Most other sorts produce only one or, in some cases, two pods per stem so that the increase in crop potential is obvious—and have you ever had too many peas? On good ground, it is also quick-growing, the peas being ready to pick 75 days after sowing.

Even more economic, perhaps, is the Asparagus Pea, which you can cook as you do beans, so that the pods are not wasted. But they must be picked when about an inch long; if left until they are larger they can be stringy.

Do you like Sweet Corn? It is rapidly increasing in popularity, particularly now that we have a variety, called Early Xtra Sweet (inset C), which is as easy to grow in this country as a lettuce and is as sweet as the best garden pea. And it should be ready for picking in three months.

HOLLY—GROW YOUR OWN DECORATION

DO YOU ever think about how some of the customs we have in Britain have been handed down from generation to generation? For instance, there is the practice of decorating our homes with holly at Christmas.

This goes right back to the days of the Romans when they used to send branches of holly to friends along with New Year gifts and good wishes.

Then in Christian times the practice was adopted and churches were decorated with holly as a sign of good will. That word "holly," some people believe, is a contraction for holy tree.

Holly, along with mistletoe and the Christmas tree, is very much a part of our traditional Christmas and folklore.

Some country folk think it is unlucky to take holly into the house before Christmas Eve.

In parts of England people refer to prickly holly as the "he" kind and the non-prickly as "she" holly. In the Midlands they take this a step further by insisting that whatever kind of holly you take into your house at Christmas will determine whether husband or wife will be boss in the year ahead. . . . You have been warned.

Yet these strange beliefs are partially borne out by fact. There are distinct "he" and "she" hollies and they make absolutely marvellous shrubs for the garden.

They will grow in ordinary soil in sun or shade. The "green" kinds as opposed to those with silver or golden leaves, will tolerate atmospheric pollution in the most heavy industrialised areas; they will withstand salt-laden winds in coastal districts, and in windy gardens, they can provide shelter for more delicate plants.

Only the "she" hollies produce berries. So much for the idea that one can tell what the weather is going to be like by the number of berries produced. . . Female hollies will produce abundant berries *every* year, if a male is planted close by. But more about that later.

Let us take a look at what the holly family (Ilex aquifolium) has to offer. "Ladies" first. For they produce the splendid berries which brighten up our houses and gardens on the darkest days.

Silver Sentinel is most beautiful with deep evergreen leaves, mottled pale green and grey with creamy yellow margins. Camelliifolia is especially noted for its extraordinarily large red berries and purple stems. Its leaves are rather special too: reddish purple when young and a rich glossy green when mature.

Whoever gave the next holly its name, really got it wrong—Golden King. This is one of the best *female* variegated hollies. The leaves are a marbled green with bright yellow margins.

Then there is Handsworth New Silver, with purple stems and green leaves, mottled grey and edged with white.

And on a dull winter's day the canary yellow and gold

leaves of the Moonlight Holly (Flavescens) are a real joy.

Not all female hollies have red berries. Those of Bacciflava are a bright yellow. Nor are all bushes upright. The variety called Pendula produces an elegant, dense weeping mound of stems clothed with silver edged green leaves and scarlet berries. All of these "she" hollies, if they are to give of their best, require a male companion.

The oldest of all garden hollies in cultivation is the male Hedgehog Holly (Ferox) which is so called because its leaves are arched and prickly like the back of a hedgehog on the defensive.

There is a form with rich purple stems and creamy-white and green leaves (Ferox argentea) and a variety with gold and yellowish green leaves (Ferox aurea). Remember that being "he" hollies, neither produces berries.

Next another couple of male hollies which are oddly named. Silver Queen and Golden Queen. Wouldn't you think someone would have the decency to rename them?

Still, they are excellent shrubs for brightening up the garden. Silver Queen has purple shoots and leaves that are marbled grey and edged with white; Golden Queen has reddish shoots and pale grey and green leaves with broad yellow margins.

More than 100 years ago that famous naturalist Charles Darwin wrote: "I have examined many hollies, but I have never found one that was really hermaphrodite."

Well, if Mr. Darwin had been alive today I would have been delighted to show him at least two hermaphrodite hollies—that is ones which are both male *and* female like many other plants.

The first is J. C. van Tol with dark, glistening and almost spineless green leaves and masses of red berries. The second is Pyramidalis with its bright green leaves, some with prickles and others without, and lots of red berries. The variety Pyramidalis fructuluteo has yellow berries.

These particular hollies will produce berries on their own. So if you have room for only one, choose a hermaphrodite. However, if you have the space available, do consider an eye-catching mixture of at least one "he" and several "she" hollies.

All the hollies which I have mentioned are slow growing. They will take ten years to reach 6 ft. with a 4 ft. spread and they can be limited in size by trimming to shape in July or August.

The varieties with dark green leaves are the toughest and will thrive in shade and in the most windswept positions. The variegated types with their gold and silver leaves need some sunshine to bring out their colours and some shelter if they are to give of their best.

All the hollies make magnificent shrubs for tubs on terraces and patios. They also make thick and colourful hedges, but remember for a berrying hedge you will need a marriage of males and females.

The individual bushes for hedges should be set out 2ft. apart in April or May. No trimming is required, but the following spring the growing tips should be removed to encourage bushy growth. April is, in fact, the time for the annual trimming of holly hedges. As with all evergreens planted in spring, the new hollies will require to be watered copiously whenever the weather is dry.

INDEX